Generations of Success

A Photographic History of Kansas State University
1863-2013

Generations of Success

A Photographic History of Kansas State University

1863-2013

By
Cliff Hight and Anthony R. Crawford

with the assistance of
Jane E. Schillie and David D. Vail

Dust jacket front: Agriculture Field Day at Kansas State, 1911.

The Donning Company Publishers
184 Business Park Drive, Suite 206
Virginia Beach, VA 23462

Steve Mull, General Manager
Barbara Buchanan, Office Manager
Anne Burns, Editor
Nathan Stufflebean, Graphic Designer
Kathy Adams, Imaging Artist
Katie Gardner, Project Research Coordinator
Tonya Washam, Research and Marketing Supervisor
Pamela Engelhard, Marketing Advisor

Barry Haire, Project Director

Library of Congress Cataloging-in-Publication Data

Hight, Cliff.
Generations of success : a photographic history of Kansas State University, 1863-2013 / by Cliff Hight and Anthony R. Crawford with the assistance of Jane E. Schillie and David D. Vail.
    pages cm
Includes bibliographical references and index.
ISBN 978-1-57864-842-9
1. Kansas State University--History--Pictorial works. I. Title.
LD2668.K58 2013
378.781'28--dc23

                            2013026668

Printed in the United States of America at Walsworth Publishing Company

Table of Contents

Foreword

Kansas State University has reached a milestone—its sesquicentennial or 150 years as Kansas's first public university and the nation's first land-grant institution to open its doors.

Our history consists of a century and a half of great efforts by K-Staters who have helped make the university what it is today. Our predecessor, Kansas State Agricultural College, was founded February 16, 1863, fewer than eight months after President Abraham Lincoln signed the Morrill Land-Grant Act.

A land-grant institution is one that champions learning, discovery, and engagement. In the past, this meant sharing knowledge that helped farmers and homemakers become more innovative and efficient, as well as an emphasis on military training. Although ROTC is no longer required of male students, the program, which now welcomes women, plays a vital role as we strive to become the nation's most military-inclusive university.

Currently, there is even more to upholding the land-grant mission. This mission is about providing all qualified students the opportunity to be part of a premier undergraduate experience unlike any in the nation. This mission is about making discoveries that inspire our imagination as to what is possible. Most of all, the land-grant mission ensures that what we've invested in Kansas State University education and research comes back to us with measurable results. K-State Research and Extension, through its presence in each Kansas county, still shares research that benefits the agriculture industry and families. Today that knowledge can encompass topics ranging from sustainable energy and programs to combating childhood obesity.

At the present time, Kansas State University offers 250 majors among nine colleges, on three campuses, with offices in Vietnam, Australia, and China—an ever-evolving university that embraces the dynamic world we serve.

Our discoveries also are making a difference across the nation and around the world. Considering the land-grant mission's global implications is imperative as we strive to become a Top 50 public research university by 2025.

Generations of Success: A Photographic History of Kansas State University, 1863–2013 presents a visual record of our impressive land-grant legacy. The book traces K-State's remarkable heritage through fascinating images, including many from the university's archives. More recent photographs capture the Wildcat spirit for present and future generations.

Please join us in celebrating 150 years of success.

Kirk H. Schulz
President
Kansas State University

Preface

In 1859, Washington Marlatt wrote Isaac Goodnow, one of his colleagues instrumental in Bluemont Central College's founding, offering some words of encouragement: "Colleges are not the growth of a *year*, but a *century*."[1] Although Marlatt was speaking about the current travails of constructing Bluemont College, his observation highlights how Kansas State University has grown to influence succeeding generations for 150 years.

As Kansas State University celebrates its sesquicentennial, we present *Generations of Success: A Photographic History of Kansas State University, 1863–2013* that captures our exciting legacy. With over five hundred images, as well as historical essays and other information, the book is divided into six chapters to provide a glimpse into Kansas State's storied past. Cliff Hight authored the introductory essays and selected the photographs for Chapters 1 thru 3. Anthony R. Crawford did the same for Chapters 4 thru 6. At the end of each introduction is a list of sources used in writing the narration. Readers wishing to learn more can consult the selected bibliography and chronology at the end of the book.

Chapter 1, "Building a Land-Grant College, 1863–1897," covers the presidencies of Joseph Denison, John Anderson, and George Fairchild. In these formative years, the college moved to a new location, developed courses in the applied sciences, and designed an agricultural experiment station.

Chapter 2, "Divisions and Milestones, 1897–1917," addresses the administrations of Thomas Will, Ernest R. Nichols, and Henry Waters. During this era, Kansas State experienced the effects of populism, developed experiment stations and extension services, and became involved in World War I.

Chapter 3, "Hardship and Opportunity, 1918–1943," shows how presidents William Jardine and Frances David Farrell handled challenges as the country dealt with World War I, the Great Depression, and World War II. Extension opportunities grew, student organizations multiplied, and research expanded across the state.

Chapter 4, "Becoming a Modern University, 1943–1975," traces Kansas State's transformation from a college to a university. A new comprehensive plan under President Milton Eisenhower revised the curriculum to meet nationally recognized higher education standards. Following Eisenhower, President James McCain continued building rigorous academic and research programs.

Chapter 5, "Advancement and Expansion, 1975–2009," focuses on presidents Duane Acker and Jon Wefald. Acker's administration upgraded Kansas State's academic programs, international presence, and campus infrastructure. Wefald's administration saw increasing enrollments, higher student achievements, successful athletic programs, and expanded campus facilities.

Chapter 6, "Initiating a New Generation, 2009–2013," describes Kansas State's new direction under President Kirk Schulz. Through his leadership, the university has embarked on an ambitious plan—K-State 2025—to become one of the nation's top fifty public research universities. Record enrollments, new programs and partnerships, and impressive athletic achievements are highlights of his administration.

Selecting photographs was an exciting yet challenging process, running the gamut from very few photographs for the first twenty-five years of Kansas State's history to the current situation whereby thousands of digital images are decentralized in locations across campus. In between, college historian Julius Willard collected a large amount of photographs from offices and individuals when he wrote his 1940 history of Kansas State. By the time the University Archives was formally established in 1983, a collection of photographs had been deposited in the library, especially from Student Publications and the *Royal Purple* yearbook. Since then, the photographic services and university news departments gave a large body of images to the University Archives, which was most helpful. Many other campus units have likewise transferred images to the University Archives, some of which fit a unique space in the book. Other collections used include photograph albums and personal collections donated by alumni and their descendants.

Although an impressive number of photographs have been preserved, there are still gaps in Kansas State's photographic record. These circumstances, along with the constraints of publication, preclude the opportunity to represent every academic unit, program, building, event, and student activity. Nevertheless, we have made every effort to include images, captions, and essays that fairly represent the overall growth and development of Kansas State in an interesting, educational, and enjoyable manner.

Unless otherwise noted in the captions, images came from the University Archives. Abbreviations used when crediting photographs include: DM-C&M for David Mayes, Division of Communications and Marketing; MB-C&M for Matt Binter, Division of Communications and Marketing; and RP for *Royal Purple* yearbooks.

Because the university has had three different names over the course of 150 years, we have used them in the following ways: "Kansas State" for the chapter introductions, KSAC (Kansas State Agricultural College) for captions that cover 1863–1931, KSC (Kansas State College) for captions that cover 1931–1959, and KSU (Kansas State University) for captions that cover 1959 to the present.

Many contributors helped us successfully complete this book. We are especially grateful to President Kirk Schulz for his excellent foreword that highlights the university's sesquicentennial and land-grant legacy. Equal gratitude goes to Bonnie Lynn-Sherow for her insightful introduction. Thanks also to Jackie Hartman and Megan Umscheid of the president's office and Sesquicentennial Steering Committee for providing institutional support at crucial moments.

Kenny Lannou shared images from K-State Athletics. David Mayes, university photographer, and Matt Binter, assistant photographer, from the Division of Communications and Marketing were integral partners. We truly appreciate David's cooperation and assistance, as he provided engaging photographs of President Schulz's first four years.

Many staff members in the Richard L. D. and Marjorie J. Morse Department of Special Collections helped with this project. Jane Schillie and David Vail provided significant and insightful research, writing, and editorial assistance. Cindy Von Elling scanned hundreds of images, greatly enhancing them. Roger Adams and Pat Patton contributed research assistance and suggestions. David Allen, who heads the Morse Department of Special Collections, provided steadfast support throughout the process. Several very talented student assistants, including Elizabeth Symm, Ian Howard, Jordan Herman, Kari Bingham, Allison Skees, and Laura Gonzales, diligently tracked down information and images. Those who assisted us deserve credit for their worthwhile contributions to *Generations of Success*, but we take full responsibility for any errors.

We extend our gratitude to editor Anne Burns and graphic designer Nathan Stufflebean at the Donning Company Publishers. Both were instrumental in producing this book. Also, special thanks to our families and friends for their steady encouragement throughout the project.

It's our pleasure to provide this photographic history in celebration of Kansas State University's sesquicentennial anniversary. We hope you enjoy the book.

Cliff Hight, University Archivist
Anthony R. Crawford, Curator of Manuscripts
Richard L. D. and Marjorie J. Morse Department of Special Collections
Kansas State University Libraries

April 9, 2013

1. Marlatt to Goodnow, 14 September 1859, Washington Marlatt papers, Morse Department of Special Collections, Kansas State University Libraries, Manhattan, Kansas. Emphasis in the original.

Introduction

"Intelligence to those who will esteem it"
Kansas State University and the Land-Grant College System

The evening of July 2, 1863, was bright with stars as an enthusiastic crowd gathered in Manhattan, Kansas, to celebrate the opening of the nation's first operational land-grant school, Kansas State Agricultural College. A thousand miles to the east, Union and Confederate soldiers lay exhausted from a second day of battle near Gettysburg, Pennsylvania. In spite of an increasingly bloody Civil War, college supporters in Manhattan trusted in the power of public education to heal and transform the nation. One hundred and fifty years later, Kansas State University remains the quintessential example of one of the most consequential and constructive federal programs ever implemented in the United States.

Signed into law on July 2, 1862, by President Abraham Lincoln, the Morrill Act gave thirty thousand acres of public land for each representative and senator in every state to establish a fund for the "endowment, support, and maintenance of at least one college where the leading object shall be, without excluding other scientific and classical studies, and including military tactics, to teach such branches of learning as are related to agriculture and the mechanic arts…in order to promote the liberal and practical education of the industrial classes in the several pursuits and professions in life." The Kansas legislature voted to accept the conditions of the Morrill Act on February 3, 1863. Two weeks later, on Monday, February 16, the legislature accepted Blue Mont Central College Association's offer to cede their college building, library, and apparatus to the state for use as a land-grant college.

Like the Emancipation Proclamation, the Homestead Act, and the creation of the United States Department of Agriculture (also passed in 1862), the Morrill Act was a bold investment in the future that marked the end of what Lincoln called the "Old Union" and the birth of a new democratic order focused on the welfare of "The People." In 1860, less than 6 percent of the adult male population of the United States had access to a college education. Representative Justin Morrill of Vermont argued that the nation could no longer afford to keep its citizens, most of whom were farmers, from the scientific knowledge they needed to reach their full potential and fulfill the nation's destiny: "Pass this measure and we shall have done—something to enable the farmer to raise two blades of grass instead of one; something for every owner of land; something for all who desire to own land; something for cheap scientific education; something for every man who loves intelligence and not ignorance."

Morrill correctly predicted the land grants would fuel national prosperity well into the future. Without education, he said, the nation's farmers were forced to glean their knowledge "from the crevices between labor and sleep. They grope in twilight." Equally prescient were the provisions that gave women and non-whites access to the land grants. Fulfilling this vision, twenty-six men and twenty-six women enrolled at the former Blue Mont College building on September 2, 1863, prompting the first Kansas State president Joseph Denison to herald the arrival of "full educational privileges." Even though enrollment was open to all students regardless of gender, race, or creed, another generation would pass before the first African-American man and woman, George Washington Owens (1899) and Minnie Howell (1901), received their Kansas State diplomas.

Congress's desire to promote prosperity and stability was a primary objective in providing classes in agriculture and the mechanical arts for the hardworking sons and daughters of the soil. As Kansas State President George Fairchild told the class of 1893, "The bulk of good work in the world—discovery, invention, government, philanthropy…is brought about by those who learn to think by study." The Hatch Act of 1887 expanded on this vision, establishing a network of agricultural experiment stations that enabled researchers to share their findings with local farmers. In addition, the Smith-Lever Act of 1914 provided county agents whose extension work proved invaluable in meeting the challenges of providing food during World War I. Together, the Morrill, Hatch, and Smith-Lever Acts provided the central architecture of the land-grant college system: teaching, research, and service.

Providing a science-based education designed to serve the needs of the general population was an enormous task in 1863. Specialists in scientific agriculture and the mechanical arts were difficult to find until the colleges themselves began to graduate their own researchers and teachers. In Kansas, as in other states, high school graduation was not required for admission until 1919. Even then, classes ranged widely from agricultural short courses of only six weeks leading to a "diploma" to full-fledged baccalaureate degrees. Finding and keeping qualified faculty was a high priority for the college from the start. As President H. J. Waters remarked in 1909, there was no need to settle for faculty who were "too good to fire and too poor to keep." The primary strength of the land-grant system was its network of scientists, many of whom attended graduate school together and then continued to share the results of their organizational and scientific endeavors. Kansas State recruited some of the very best agricultural scientists of the day, becoming a leading research school in a number of economically important crops as well as ecology and home economics.

To aid the state's public schools, coursework in teacher education was offered in 1900 to help train teachers in rural districts. By 1914, in keeping with the expansion of public schools nationally, Kansas State created a separate department of education. Equally important, Kansas State's curriculum in the first half of the twentieth century was the remarkable presence of the dean of women, Mary Van Zile, and the dean of home economics, Helen Thompson, whose unflagging organizational work during the flu epidemic of 1918 saved hundreds of lives both on and off campus. Today, Kansas State University has more buildings named for women than any other land-grant college in the United States (Van Zile, Thompson, Justin, Kramer, Kedzie, and Calvin).

In spite of meager appropriations and economic depression in the 1920s and 1930s, the campus expanded dramatically in size and numerous new buildings were constructed to meet the needs of a growing student population. In 1934, President Farrell commissioned a twenty-year plan for the college that made clear it was better to concentrate on its traditional curricula: "It will strengthen its work in agriculture, engineering, and the physical and biological sciences.... It will develop vertically rather than horizontally." As always, the primary mission of the school was educating the average Kansas student who otherwise might not have the opportunity to attend college.

The next major expansion at Kansas State was initiated by the passage of the GI Bill of Rights that paved the way for the veterans of World War II, the majority of whom were the first in their families to attend college. The original colleges and programs at Kansas State remained strong, but the Morrill Act also provided for the "liberal and practical education of the industrial classes in the several pursuits and professions in life." Farrell's 1934 plan for "growing vertically" ended with the appointment of Milton Stover Eisenhower in 1943. While the primary reason for change was, once again, a world war, Eisenhower's national and international perspective on the future of public education propelled Kansas State into becoming a model postwar campus. Although fully occupied with the immediate needs of the war, Eisenhower noted in his 1944 biennial report to the Regents that "military victory alone will not achieve the great objectives for which this war is being fought." One of those objectives was a broader and more inclusive educational program that prepared students to be leaders, not just in their communities but in the world at large. To fund that vision, a non-profit endowment was established by Eisenhower to solicit private gifts to the school. After decades of steady and sometimes decreased enrollments, the student population began to swell, from a record five thousand in 1946–1947 to eight thousand in 1947–1948. Rules governing student behavior were relaxed and the first woman was elected president of the student governing association, Ethelinda Parrish, the daughter of beloved history professor Fred L. Parrish. At a time when the citizens of Manhattan were attempting to maintain the color line in public schools and services, Eisenhower made it clear he supported the integration of the school, in keeping with the original intent of the Morrill Act to provide access to all citizens regardless of race.

As the United States rose to prominence as a world power so did the People's colleges. The creation of modern student loan programs marked an enormous expansion in federal support for higher education. As in other land-grant schools, the college acknowledged its expanded role in 1959 by changing its name to Kansas State University of Agriculture and Applied Science; quickly shortened in practice to Kansas State University. Renewed support for universities was widely embraced as a needed investment in the future and Kansas State quickly rose to the challenge. The number of faculty with terminal degrees jumped significantly as did their accomplishments. Under the postwar guidance of Kansas State President Eisenhower, the curriculum embraced the humanities, business, and architecture. The nation's land-grant schools moved ever closer to the Jeffersonian ideal of the "diffusion of knowledge…for the preservation of freedom and happiness," not just in the United States but across the globe.

While maintaining its open admissions policy to all Kansas high school graduates, new and revitalized programs in education, journalism, architecture, veterinary medicine, and engineering as well as dozens of graduate programs in traditional fields elevated the expectations of both students and faculty at Kansas State. Under the leadership of President Jon Wefald, Kansas State students became known for their unparalleled success in winning international and national scholarships such as the Rhodes, Truman, Marshall, Udall, and Goldwater. Energetic recruitment efforts aimed at the state's high school population led to a majority of Kansas residents choosing Kansas State over other schools. Pride in the achievements of the school and the passage of Title IX funding supported a needed renaissance in school athletics including the construction of new facilities for football, basketball, and fitness. In 1990, Kansas State students led the nation in the percentage who participated in intramural sports programs. A tradition of shared governance between administration, faculty, and students made possible construction of over two million square feet of classroom, laboratory, and library space. External research funding also reached unprecedented levels, from $19 million in 1986 to over $150 million in 2012. Together with its continued support for a statewide network of experiment stations, branch campuses at Salina and Olathe, and now international agreements with universities in China, India, Vietnam, Afghanistan, and Australia, Kansas State remains true to its original mission of the dissemination of knowledge through research, teaching, and service for the benefit of all.

In 1862, only one young man in 1,500 attended college. Today, more than 4.5 million students attend sixty-nine land-grant schools. Throughout the country, public colleges are a mainstay of the economy as engines of technological and creative innovation. Nationally, two-thirds of all federal funds for research are awarded to faculty in public universities. Most important, federal support for higher education has stayed true to the belief that an educated populace is the safeguard of democracy. A century and a half following Representative Morrill's plea for "useful knowledge…in order to enlarge our productive power [and] give intelligence to those who will esteem it," land-grant schools and Kansas State University remain central to the enduring ideals of the American Republic.

Bonnie Lynn-Sherow
Associate Professor of History
Director of the Chapman Center for Rural Studies
Kansas State University

Chapter 1
Building a Land-Grant College,
1863–1897

Topeka photographer J. R. Riddle took this view of the KSAC campus in 1885 from the area known today as Aggieville.

Kansas State's beginnings are indelibly linked with the founding of Manhattan, Kansas. Settlers came to the area in the 1850s, many from New England and Ohio. Most from the northeast were abolitionists attached to the New England Emigrant Aid Company, while those from Ohio were Free-Staters from the Cincinnati and Kansas Land Company who arrived aboard the steamboat *Hartford*. From the beginning, Manhattan was "considered one of the sturdiest and most uncompromising of the Free-State outposts."[1]

Many of the settlers were also interested in higher education, and during their travels to Kansas some discussed establishing a college at the new settlement. In April 1855, a citizen approached the community's trustees with ideas for an agricultural school—which Kansas State historian Julius T. Willard recognized "as the beginning of Kansas State." However, the educational institution preceding it was Bluemont Central College, which provided a primary and preparatory education to about 150 students from 1860 to 1863.[2] This Methodist school was chartered by the Kansas Territorial Legislature and resided on the northwest corner of the present-day intersection of College Avenue and Claflin Road.

Bluemont Central College's organization included a literary department and an agricultural department, a combination that reflected the philosophical evolution of agricultural education since the previous century—mixing classical education with industrial training. Concurrent with the school's genesis, U.S. Representative Justin Morrill of Vermont was advocating congressional passage of his land-grant act to provide financial resources to educate the industrial classes. Vetoed in 1858, it became law in 1862, providing the legal framework for the transfer of Bluemont Central College from private to public hands.

Bluemont supporters included, left to right: Washington Marlatt (principal), Robert L. Harford (teacher and trustee), Joseph Denison (trustee), Joseph G. Schnebly (KSAC professor), Isaac T. Goodnow (trustee, fundraiser).

George S. Park

Samuel D. Houston

John Kimball

Samuel Pomeroy

Staunch supporters of Bluemont Central College (precursor to KSAC) took an idea proposed by early settler George S. Park to establish an agricultural school near Manhattan and made it a reality. After obtaining a charter in 1858 from the state legislature, promoters began efforts to raise funds for the college. Park gave $500 before leaving Manhattan, early settler Samuel D. Houston donated $300, and young local farmer John Kimball contributed $200. Washington Marlatt, Joseph Denison, and Isaac T. Goodnow were the most visible proponents of the school. In addition to their financial contributions, they helped with construction, fundraising, recruiting, and instruction. In May 1859, about three hundred people attended the cornerstone dedication, at which founding trustee Samuel Pomeroy and others spoke. In January 1860, Bluemont Central College opened its doors.

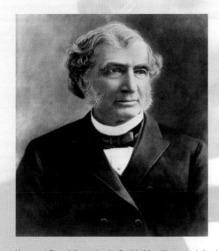

Vermont Republican Justin Smith Morrill penned the legislation that granted federal lands for states to establish agricultural colleges. He served in the United States House (1855–1867) and Senate (1867–1898). He also sponsored the Agricultural College Act of 1890 that provided additional funding to land-grant colleges.

Isaac Goodnow's involvement with Kansas State started before its inception in 1863. As he ended his years of service, he reported, "From the first the College has been [my] *pet child*."[3] Like a doting father, Goodnow had labored for more than a decade to give the developing land-grant institution in Manhattan as much as he could to ensure its success.

This undated photograph shows the Bluemont Central College building with people in front and in the windows. To help finance its construction, Isaac Goodnow campaigned for funds in the eastern United States. Notable contributors included poet Henry Wadsworth Longfellow and former Harvard president Jared Sparks. Built with local limestone, the three-story structure had over 7,000 square feet, the largest educational building in the Kansas territory.

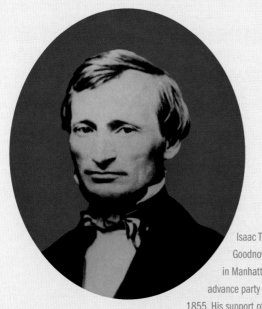

Isaac Tichenor Goodnow arrived in Manhattan with an advance party of settlers in 1855. His support of education included serving in many capacities at Bluemont Central College, as state superintendent of public instruction, and as KSAC land agent. He remained involved in civic and educational affairs in the region until his death in 1894.

The West Troy, New York, foundry of A. Meneely's Sons mailed Goodnow a $250 estimate to forge the 513-pound college bell. Goodnow convinced Massachusetts philanthropist Joseph Ingalls to finance the project. Installed in 1861, the bell's peals carried five miles. It eventually rang from Anderson Hall until 1965 and now is a monument in front of Bluemont Hall.

Kansas State Agricultural College opened in 1863, becoming the first newly created land-grant college following the passage of the Morrill Act. On February 16, shortly after approving the legislature's resolution to accept the act, Governor Thomas Carney agreed to their resolution to receive the Bluemont Central College trustees' offer of their building and one hundred acres of land for the creation of a state agricultural college. Bluemont Central College had been facing financial uncertainty and inconsistent enrollment, and its transfer to the state ensured a more sustainable future. Designed to fiscally strengthen agricultural colleges by providing federal lands to states for public sale, the provisions of the Morrill Act gave Kansas 90,000 acres. A land agent began selling this acreage in early 1866, and within twenty-five years total sales eclipsed $500,000.

Joseph Denison transitioned from the presidency of Bluemont Central College to being president of Kansas State from 1863 to 1873. With enrollment doubling during Kansas State's initial decade, Denison led efforts to accommodate the growth by relocating campus one mile eastward. The move required collaboration with Manhattan's leaders to purchase much of the present-day campus. Also, in accordance with Kansas State's land-grant mission, his administration created farmers' and agricultural institutes to share agricultural knowledge with Kansans.

Despite these efforts, Denison's administration struggled to provide appropriate personnel and curriculum, such as not having an agriculture professor until 1868. There was a limited candidate pool, as all land-grant colleges experienced. Another difficulty was balancing classical curriculum with industrial education. Coursework included algebra, astronomy, botany, chemistry, philosophy, Greek, and Latin. Later courses included more agricultural and mechanical classes, but a new administration was necessary to implement a more focused program for agriculture and applied sciences.

Goodnow's brother-in-law, Joseph Denison, shared his enthusiasm for education. Denison was president of three Kansas schools: Bluemont Central College (1863), Kansas State Agricultural College (1863-1873), and Baker University (1874–1879). His leadership and vision guided KSAC through its first decade, graduating fifteen of more than one thousand students who attended during his tenure.

Manhattan's main street, shown here in about 1865, highlighted the town's frontier heritage. Surviving Bleeding Kansas, serious drought, and the Civil War, Manhattan soon would connect with rail and telegraph service and quickly become a microcosm of agriculture, industry, and college life in the American West.

Jeremiah E. Platt joined KSAC's faculty in 1864 as head of the preparatory department and professor of vocal music. As he served during Denison's, Anderson's, and Fairchild's presidencies, his teaching responsibilities changed to elementary education and mathematics. In 1883, despite student protest, the Board of Regents asked Platt for his resignation, likely for his support of prohibition.

Elbridge Gale was a college regent (1864–1871) and horticulturalist and nursery superintendent (1871–1878) who sold his farm to KSAC in 1871. His involvement in farmers' institutes and other service activities increased his reputation throughout Kansas as an expert on trees. After leaving the college, he lost the 1878 election for U.S. Representative to KSAC President John Anderson.

In 1865, state geologist Benjamin Franklin Mudge became KSAC's professor of natural science. A passionate teacher, Mudge taught more than ten subjects and was well liked by students. Unfortunately, the Board of Regents dismissed him in 1874 for protesting the nominations of new Regents.

Belle Haines

Emma Haines's Diploma

Belle and Emma Haines were members of KSAC's first class, graduating in 1867. The sisters were the first of five generations of Haines family members who have attended KSAC. Belle assisted in the preparatory department as a student, and in 1898 her son Raymond became the first child of a graduate to complete a KSAC degree. Emma was an active alumna who encouraged other graduates to stay connected to college events. She also wrote a short autobiography essay, "Then, or Fifty Years Ago," that described her childhood and time at KSAC.

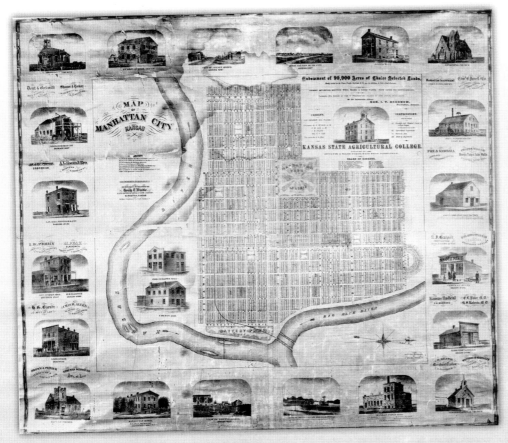

This map shows Manhattan, Kansas, in 1867. Around the map are images of town businesses and churches, and on the upper right is information about KSAC and public lands for sale. Isaac Goodnow was the land agent at the time.

John S. Hougham was KSAC's first professor of agriculture from 1868 to 1872. His appointment came after President Joseph Denison had searched five years for a qualified candidate. Although not an experienced farmer, Hougham acquired livestock and plants for study and practice at KSAC before becoming a professor at Purdue University in 1872.

Henry J. Detmers, first professor of veterinary science and animal husbandry at KSAC, taught from 1872 to 1874. A German immigrant, Detmers also taught German at KSAC. Like Benjamin F. Mudge, the Board of Regents dismissed Detmers in 1874 for protesting the nominations of new Regents.

Renowned entomologist Charles Valentine Riley lectured at KSAC in the 1870s, receiving an honorary master of arts degree in 1873. In the 1930s, Riley's widow donated some of his insect drawings to KSC, which are now in the university archives.

When John Anderson became president in 1873, he shelved much of the classical curriculum and emphasized applied sciences, naming the courses farmer's, mechanic's, and woman's. University historian Willard recognized that Anderson "was extreme; that he was ultra-practical, and failed to see the real value of much of what is too lightly stigmatized as theoretical. Nevertheless, the times required his iconoclastic work to tear the college completely loose from the bonds of traditional education, and to place it squarely in a new setting where it has since remained." What historian James Carey termed as "Anderson's hammer-and-tongs approach" created much discussion in the college community.[4] Although the president's efforts to train students in industrial fields definitely aligned with the Morrill Act goal of educating the farming and laboring classes, he neglected its associated purpose to instruct students in scientific and classical studies.

Nevertheless, Anderson successfully completed the campus move that Denison began, with most college activities occurring there by 1879. One of Anderson's most important achievements was his introduction of a college newspaper, *The Industrialist*, which improved communication with students, alumni, and citizens and provided a vehicle for Anderson to spread his industrial education perspective. Well liked by students, he also was popular with Kansans. In fact, his presidency ended in 1879 following his election to the U.S. House of Representatives. Although contemporaries debated the effects of Anderson's efforts, his legacy of curriculum revision, continued campus development, and a greater statewide educational presence was irrefutable.[5]

John A. Anderson was KSAC's second president (1873–1879) and previously had been a Presbyterian minister in Junction City, Kansas. He believed land-grant education should focus on practical agriculture, mechanics, and homemaking with little attention to classical or liberal arts courses. Students found him approachable, although some faculty members bristled at his abrupt shift in educational emphasis. In 1878, Anderson ran successfully for a seat in the U.S. House of Representatives and resigned as KSAC president in 1879.

One of President Anderson's most important accomplishments was supporting the college's first newspaper, *The Industrialist*. First published on April 24, 1875, the paper's expressed purpose was to "promote the liberal and practical education of the industrial classes in their several pursuits." Faculty and administrators were the earliest contributors, and eventually the publication focused on alumni until its print run ended in 1955.

Male and female students of varied ages assisted in KSAC's printing office on the second floor of the Shops building (part of present-day Seaton Complex) in about 1888. President Anderson introduced printing curriculum in 1873, and by the time of this photograph they were printing *The Industrialist* newspaper and other campus publications.

Julius Terrass Willard entered KSAC as a student in 1879 and remained associated with the college for the next seventy years, other than ten months he spent in graduate study at Johns Hopkins University. In addition to receiving undergraduate and graduate degrees from KSAC, he was student assistant, instructor, professor, chemist for both the Agricultural Experiment Station and the Engineering Experiment Station, vice director and director of the Agricultural Experiment Station, head of the chemistry department, dean of general science, vice president, acting president (twice), and college historian. In 1950, he died at his desk in Anderson Hall at the age of eighty-eight. Willard was portrayed here by Manhattan photographer F. W. Amos in 1901.

The original north wing of Anderson Hall, built in 1879, is visible on the left side of this early view of campus. It had classrooms for English, drawing, mathematics, and practical agriculture, as well as space for cloakrooms, the president's office, and the library. Alumnus William Ulrich was the successful bidder to cut the stone for the building. Every president since George Fairchild has had his office somewhere in Anderson Hall (Image from 1877–1878 *Biennial Report of the State Board of Agriculture*).

STATE AGRICULTURAL COLLEGE, MANHATTAN.
(From a photograph taken on top of Rev E. Gale's dwelling.)

The chemistry department occupied this building from its construction in 1876 until 1900. The design incorporated the latest European ideas for laboratories and included an elaborate ventilation system that utilized windows flanking the cupola. An accidental fire in 1900 nearly destroyed the building, and after massive renovation it became the women's gymnasium. It later housed chemistry and math classes until 1963 when it was named for men's advisor Adrian A. Holtz. Since then, many different student-oriented services and programs have been based there.

J. D. Walters taught industrial art, design, and architecture at KSAC from 1877 to 1917. He drew architectural plans for some of the campus buildings and was instrumental in developing the architecture program. During President Thomas Will's administration, Walters effectively managed the college bookstore and was one of his most vocal supporters. In 1909, KSAC published his *History of the Kansas State Agricultural College.* Upon retirement, Walters became an emeritus professor.

Milan L. Ward was a KSAC professor from 1873 to 1883, teaching math, English, and engineering courses. In addition, he had stints as the loan commissioner for the Board of Regents (1875–1883), college librarian (1880–1882), and acting president when Anderson ran for Congress in 1878. Like Professor Platt, the Board of Regents asked Ward for his resignation in 1883, likely for his support of prohibition.

George H. Failyer was graduated from KSAC in 1877 and returned to campus to teach chemistry, physics, mineralogy, and geology from 1878 to 1897. He also served on campus agricultural committees that oversaw the implementation of extension services and farm institutes.

The Shops building and Horticulture Hall were built in 1875 and 1876, respectively. The Shops building, now part of Seaton Complex, is the oldest remaining building on campus. It provided necessary space for students to learn vocational training such as wagon repair, carpentry, and painting. The Shops building is used today for interior architectural design and general classroom needs. Horticulture Hall once stood on present-day Coffman Commons and for thirty years was home to horticulture education. By the 1920s, the illustrations department used the building for college photographic services, including the *Royal Purple.* In 1959, the building was demolished for construction of the north wing of Eisenhower Hall.

George Thompson Fairchild was KSAC's third president, from 1879 to 1897. For the first decade of his presidency, two of his brothers were also college presidents: Edward Henry Fairchild at Berea College and James Harris Fairchild at Oberlin College. In 1896, Fairchild presided over the National Association of American Agricultural Colleges.

George Fairchild succeeded Anderson and brought a more moderate approach to land-grant education. As Willard noted, "Anderson's ideal was a splendid trade school, Fairchild's a college for persons engaged in agriculture, or preparing for occupations related to agriculture."[6] Administratively, Fairchild was democratic in his governance with weekly faculty meetings covering all college-related topics, not just discipline and scholarship issues. With curriculum, he modified early coursework to cover basic education before specializing in particular subjects. Under his leadership, Kansas State raised admission requirements, formalized graduate study, restarted farmers' institutes, developed the Agricultural Experiment Station, expanded emerging athletic and extracurricular opportunities, and added running water, electricity, steam heat, hot water, and telephones to campus.

These successes did not leave Kansas State without challenges. In the 1890s, the populist movement, which historian Eric Foner called "the era's greatest political insurgency," disrupted the college's administrative and instructional stability. Populism resonated with farmers and laborers suffering from economic insecurity, and proponents sought working-class protections, public ownership of utilities, and reductions in the concentration of

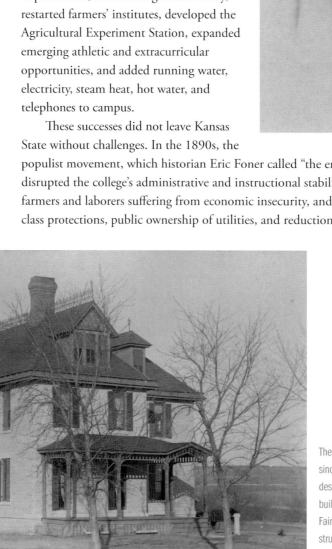

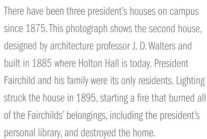

There have been three president's houses on campus since 1875. This photograph shows the second house, designed by architecture professor J. D. Walters and built in 1885 where Holton Hall is today. President Fairchild and his family were its only residents. Lighting struck the house in 1895, starting a fire that burned all of the Fairchilds' belongings, including the president's personal library, and destroyed the home.

wealth. The movement also influenced higher education—especially agricultural colleges—by instituting courses that promoted populist concepts. Contemporary Kansas State professor J. D. Walters said state Populist leaders "agreed that President Fairchild was an uncompromising Republican, an autocrat, and a man who had outlived his usefulness, that the Faculty was rusty, [and] that the College should give more attention to economic science."[7] After two Populist governors stacked the college's Board of Regents with like-minded members, the Board added more lectures on economics, removed the entire faculty in 1897 (before rehiring about two-thirds of them), and replaced President Fairchild with President Thomas Will.

Fairchild's unceremonious dismissal did not diminish his achievements. Creating a more moderate institution, Fairchild was, in Carey's words, "flexible and open to suggestion, able to accept criticism with grace and dignity."[8] His leadership, along with President Denison's and President Anderson's, helped the college make significant progress since 1863. During its formative decades, Kansas State moved from a single building on one hundred acres to a new site with six buildings on 220 acres. Kansas State provided research opportunities for faculty members and students, designed an agricultural experiment station, and developed a national reputation in areas of study that included agriculture, domestic science, engineering, and science.

— Cliff Hight

Ira Graham worked at KSAC in many capacities from 1879 to 1898, including superintendent of the telegraph department (1879-1890), college secretary (1881-1898), and professor of bookkeeping, commercial law, and accounting (1897-1898). He installed the college's first telephone exchange in 1895.

For further reading beyond the sources in the notes, see the following:

Brown, Richard D. "The Agricultural College Land Grant in Kansas: Selection and Disposal," *Agricultural History* 37:2 (April 1963), 94–102.

Willard, Julius T. "Bluemont Central College, the Forerunner of Kansas State College," *The Kansas Historical Quarterly* 13:6 (May 1945), 323–357.

1. Kevin Olson, *Frontier Manhattan: Yankee Settlement to Kansas Town, 1854-1894* (Lawrence, KS: University Press of Kansas, 2012), 4.
2. Julius Terrass Willard, *History of Kansas State College of Agriculture and Applied Science* (Manhattan, KS: Kansas State College Press, 1940), 10. Bluemont was also spelled Blue Mont at times, including in the charter. For consistency, "Bluemont" will be used throughout unless direct quotes are different. Concerning enrollment numbers, some sources differ, but it appears there were twenty-nine in January 1860, fifty-three by March 1860, fifteen in Fall 1860, twenty-five in Spring 1862, and seventy-five during the 1862–1863 school year. There are some gaps in the record, which leads to the estimated number of 150.
3. Isaac Goodnow, *Report to Board of Regents Kansas State Agricultural College*, July 16, 1873, 5. Emphasis in the original.
4. Julius Terrass Willard in *A Standard History of Kansas and Kansans*, William E. Connelly, ed., vol. 2 (Chicago: Lewis Publishing Company, 1918), 1025. James C. Carey, *Kansas State University: The Quest for Identity* (Lawrence, KS: The Regents Press of Kansas, 1977), 56.
5. For historians' perspectives of Anderson's educational efforts, see J. D. Walters, *History of the Kansas State Agricultural College* ([Manhattan, KS]: Kansas State Agricultural College Printing Department, 1909), 47–77; Willard, *History of Kansas State College of Agriculture and Applied Science*, 35–57; and Carey, *Kansas State University: The Quest for Identity*, 39–66.
6. Willard, *History of Kansas State College of Agriculture and Applied Science*, 60.
7. Eric Foner, *Give Me Liberty! An American History*, 3rd edition, vol. 2 (New York: W.W. Norton & Company, 2011), 680. Walters, *History of the Kansas State Agricultural College*, 111.
8. Carey, *Kansas State University: The Quest for Identity*, 65.

In 1886, Henrietta Willard graduated from KSAC and married John H. Calvin the next week. She returned to Kansas with her five children after John's death in 1898 and was the college librarian from 1901 to 1903 and professor of home economics from 1903 to 1908. She later worked at Purdue University, Oregon State University, and the U.S. Bureau of Education. Calvin Hall, built in 1908, was named for her in 1925.

Courses like this dairying class began after President John Anderson's 1873 curriculum reorganization and implementation of the woman's course. This class was part of the Farm Economy course that was taught in the southeast basement room in Anderson Hall.

One room inside Anderson Hall was the college secretary's office. This undated image shows the secretary (possibly Ira Graham) and an assistant performing administrative duties.

This photograph of Anderson Hall was taken shortly before the center portion was completed and the north wing was renovated in 1882. The central portion, commonly called Main College at the time, was used for various academic and administrative purposes over the years.

Above: Anderson Hall can be seen in the distance from the Vattier Street campus entrance in the 1890s. The wall and posts were built in 1872 and this opening was known as the front entrance for decades. An iron gate was used in the 1880s and early 1890s to keep errant cows off the campus.

Left: This view of Anderson Hall and the road approaching it is after a snowstorm in about 1895.

Above: A. C. McCreary served as college janitor and engineer from 1887 to 1897. Halfway through his service, he nearly suffered a three-story fall when the rope broke while he was hoisting the flag on the roof of Anderson Hall's south end. *The Industrialist* reported he was saved "by mere accident [when] his feet caught in the gutter at the eaves." McCreary was highly praised for his work, although he suffered serious neuralgia for his last five years. The affliction led to four surgeries, and he died in 1897 after complications from the final one.

Top Left: Nellie Kedzie, standing in the back of the photograph, taught this 1885 sewing class in Anderson Hall. Sewing was one of the first courses included in President Anderson's introduction of the woman's course in 1873.

Middle Left: By the time of this photograph in 1888, the KSAC library fit 8,500 volumes in the northeast corner of Anderson Hall's first floor. When the Bluemont Central College trustees made their donation to the state in 1863, the gift included a 3,000-volume library.

Left: The KSAC Board of Regents stood on the north steps of Anderson Hall for this 1892 photograph. Members included (in alphabetical order) George Fairchild, A. P. Forsyth, Harrison Kelley, Edward Secrest, E. D. Stratford, W. D. Street, and Joshua Wheeler. The Board of Regents was connected only to KSAC from 1863 until it was absorbed into a statewide Board of Administration in 1913.

After passage of the 1887 Hatch Act, KSAC built an agricultural experiment station for $1,950 and the adjoining propagating houses for $2,100. Located where Hale Library now stands, the office and laboratory provided additional research space for analysis of various horticultural and entomological subjects. After removing the propagating houses, KSAC used the stone building for purposes that included the state dairy commissioner's office and housing for college nurses.

The Morrill Act included a clause concerning military tactics education, and KSAC followed it from the beginning. This photograph shows some of the college battalion's stacked arms in front of the Armory (later called Farm Machinery Hall). The building was a place for drilling and training battalion members, as well as storing more than seventy rifles and two artillery pieces.

This 1888 image shows military tactics professor Lieutenant John F. Morrison leading a women's calisthenics drill. Morrison was at KSAC from 1887 to 1890 and retired from the military in 1921, having served his last four years as the U.S. Army's director of training.

The college battalion often drilled in front of the Armory, as pictured in formation here in 1888. Military instruction at KSAC began when ten students drilled under a classmate in 1863. At various times, college leaders made and lifted requirements for male students to take military training. There was no military tactics professor during the 1870s, and the following decade brought more consistent drilling.

The horticulture sub-foremen for 1890–1891 during a break: Sam Van Blarcom, Phil Creager, Frank Waugh, and George Clothier. Waugh, later a pioneer in landscape architecture, dedicated the accompanying sketch to the group.

These 1892 agriculture students were the afternoon working squad on the college farm. Another group worked the farm in the mornings.

Part of KSAC's agricultural coursework included the application of farm chemicals. This 1892 photograph of a man using a Douglas knapsack sprayer shows another way farmers could fight pests.

Here students were honing their gardening skills in the plots beside Horticulture Hall during an 1892 KSAC floriculture class.

The horticulture barn depicted here was built in 1889 and used until being razed in 1919. Located near present-day Hale Library, the stones were used to enlarge another campus building.

This 1893 photograph shows robber bees forcing their way into another beehive. The hive was located southeast of the Armory. Part of KSAC's agricultural curriculum included beekeeping and honey harvesting.

This group of veterinary science students stood outside the Armory in 1892. The class description stated that lectures were "adapted to wants of farmers and stockmen." It also mentioned "operations are performed before the class, and students are requested to assist."

A museum opened at KSAC as early as 1867 with geological specimens from Benjamin Mudge and skeletons and other items for studying anatomy and physiology. Its third location was the Armory, pictured here, between about 1884 and 1894, and collections were added including entomological, agricultural, and zoological displays. In 1894, the museum was moved to Fairchild Hall. Some of the images below, such as the boy feeding the mounted elk, are from when the museum was in Fairchild Hall.

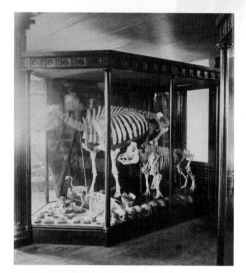

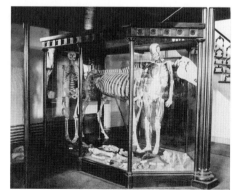

The iron shop and the foundry were built for $4,000 in 1891 to improve the quality of mechanical engineering education.

Ozni Porter Hood, seen here in his office in the Shops building, worked at KSAC from 1886 to 1898. Beginning as superintendent of shops, Hood quickly joined the faculty and contributed a great deal to the improvement of mechanical engineering with shop expansions and curriculum development. Among the more unique topics he discussed with students were the mechanics of the phonograph and using windmills for irrigation.

Students were photographed wearing smocks in the chemistry lab (present-day Holtz Hall) preparing experiments in about 1888.

Bessie "Belle" Little was an 1891 domestic science graduate, about the date this photo was taken. Returning to Manhattan after receiving her medical degree, she became the town's first female medical doctor when she started her practice in 1907. In addition to her community efforts, she was an assistant physician on campus and helped design KSAC's nursing curriculum in the 1920s and 1930s.

Music has been offered at KSAC since 1863. An orchestra became reality by 1882, and it played daily for chapel exercises in Anderson Hall. The college orchestra in this photograph, likely from 1892, included students and faculty such as music professor Alexander B. Brown (second row with beard).

(From left) Alfred Midgley, Harry Moore, John Morse, Phil Creager, Herman Avery, Kary Davis, and Sam Van Blarcom were involved in designing and producing KSAC's first yearbook, *College Symposium*. This 1891 class book included a history of the college and information about faculty and students. Published intermittently under various titles, class books were precursors of the annual *Royal Purple*, which first appeared in 1909.

KSAC's first football team pictured in 1894. While students had played football here as early as 1887, the faculty was unsupportive until this year.

Claude M. Breese, assistant in chemistry from 1887 to 1897, was photographed playing tennis on the lawn south of the Armory in 1891.

Edwin A. Popenoe, shown here playing baseball at the Manhattan city park in about 1890, was a KSAC professor from 1879 to 1897 and from 1899 to 1907. He taught botany, zoology, horticulture, and entomology and was involved in creating the Agricultural Experiment Station. In addition to running his farm near Topeka during his second stint, Popenoe was involved in many professional organizations.

The 1897 KSAC baseball team included students and community members, and it was not uncommon at that time for college teams to play local city teams or semi-professional teams from within the region. Under the leadership of H. W. Wagner, the team played seven games and won four. Names supplied on the back of the print are (front row, left to right): Frank Cheadale, Ashbrook, Leonard Poston, and Coach Wagner. Back row: Oliver Noble, Fred Dial, George Menke, Doc Wagner, Green, and Delmer Akin.

This group of students gathered for a formal portrait that included women holding a baseball and a Spalding baseball bat from the 1890s. KSAC students played baseball games as early as 1866, and the sport continued to gain popularity. Beginning in 1890, faculty and seniors played a baseball game as part of commencement day festivities.

Surveying was taught at KSAC from the beginning. This group worked with Royal S. Kellogg (second man from left), student assistant for surveying from 1894 to 1896, who earned $0.20 per hour to teach them the basics. Kellogg became a forestry pioneer who helped shape U.S. Forest Service policies during Theodore Roosevelt's presidency.

These home economics students in the 1890s displayed their cooking and food preparation skills.

Nellie Sawyer Kedzie, pictured in her office with assistant Ruth Stokes in about 1895, led home economics education at KSAC from 1882 to 1897. An 1876 graduate of KSAC, Kedzie returned to teach at her alma mater, becoming the first alumna to lead a KSAC department. She successfully lobbied for a new home economics building, which was completed in 1898 and named in her honor in 1902.

Alpha Beta Society

Hamilton Society

Ionian Society

Literary societies including those pictured here in the 1890s were integral parts of campus social life from the early years of KSAC. The Alpha Beta Literary Society was organized in 1868, but did not permit women until 1875. The men's Hamilton Literary Society started in 1884 with an emphasis on public speaking and debate. The women's Ionian Literary Society began in 1887 under the tutelage of Nellie Kedzie with the purpose of "mutual improvement and the cultivation of the forensic art, literature and music."

Construction began on Fairchild Hall in 1893 to house the library, museum, and agricultural science instruction, shown in this above photo taken from the southeast. The right image shows the completed Fairchild Hall from the southwest in 1896. Originally called Library and Science Hall, the building today houses the Graduate School, Research and Sponsored Programs, International Programs, and the Office of Student Financial Assistance.

1892 Faculty.

The *Student's Herald* reported, "The beautiful home of E. L. Knostman was the scene of a merry valentine party last Friday evening," which happened to be February 14, 1896. E. L. and his wife Mable, proprietors of Manhattan's Knostman Clothing Company and supporters of KSAC, invited students and community members to this party.

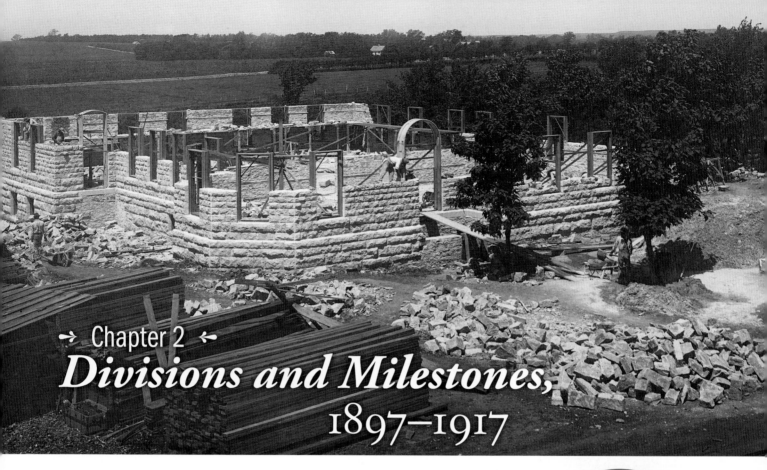

→ Chapter 2 ←
Divisions and Milestones,
1897–1917

This photograph shows the construction of the domestic science building in 1897. Completed in 1898, it was named for Nellie Kedzie in 1902 to recognize her significant contributions to the department. After many years of limited space in the basement and first floors of Anderson Hall, the new structure became the first building in the U.S. erected solely for domestic science education.

Thomas Will began his presidency at Kansas State in 1897 after the Populist-majority Board of Regents dismissed George Fairchild. To more broadly educate students in populist ideals, the Regents added economics courses that included topics such as tariffs, taxation, and public utilities. Despite the political tumult of the times, Will oversaw an improved use of faculty committees, the instigation of engineering curriculum, and experiments with a college bookstore, dining hall, and printing office.

A military milestone occurred at Kansas State in 1898. Approximately thirty students, the first students to leave Kansas State for wartime service, enlisted in a volunteer unit during the Spanish-American War. The unit trained in Virginia while awaiting orders to Cuba, but was never deployed. Since then, Kansas State students have enlisted in the United States military during nearly every major war.

Thomas Elmer Will was president of KSAC from 1897 to 1899 after starting as economics professor in 1894. At thirty-six, he remains the institution's youngest president, and his two-year administration still is the shortest in KSAC history. Will was swept into office amidst Populist reforms that were short-lived. Even those who disagreed with him praised him as "a man of unsurpassed industry, a penetrating student, and an esteemed teacher." After leaving KSAC, Will worked in academia for nearly a decade and spent the remainder of his life as an integral proponent of developing the Florida Everglades.

After the Spanish-American War ended, Kansas State was the site of an academic battle. Populists lost political clout and Republicans regained a majority in the college's Board of Regents in 1899, quickly dismissing President Will and like-minded professors in an attempt to expunge populism from the college.

Assessments of Will by Kansas State colleagues were mixed. J. D. Walters, professor of drawing and architecture, considered him "a man of unusual energy, a good organizer and a good mixer, a man who literally worked day and night."[1] However, chemistry professor Julius T. Willard believed he "lacked greatly in the ordinary man-to-man contacts of life, did not mingle congenially with his colleagues, and was sadly lacking in a sense of humor. A joke by him was a very rare product."[2] Nevertheless, Will was an energetic and tireless organizer who did much in his short tenure, but quickly became a martyr when the political tables turned.

George Washington Owens (1875–1950) became the first African-American graduate of KSAC in 1899. While a student, Owens worked on the college farm and as a janitor, contributed to the Webster Literary Society, and wrote his senior thesis on "Dairy Form as an Index to Character," which included this photograph. After graduation he worked under George Washington Carver at Tuskegee Institute in Alabama until 1907. The following year Owens went to Virginia State University and started their agriculture and agricultural extension departments. He retired as chairman of the agriculture department in 1945.

Mamie Alexander left her rural Kansas home in 1898 for Kansas State with $17.50 to her name. Her college adventure included working year-round, managing a full academic schedule, and finding time to date her future husband, Frank Boyd. She reflected on her experience, "By the end of my freshman year, I knew my own instructors and most of the others, and also knew most of the … students on the campus. Each subsequent year, Kansas State became more and more an integral part of my family."[3] Like many Kansas State students, Mamie felt strong ties to her alma mater.

The 1897–1898 faculty were involved in a great deal of transition. One-third of them had arrived at the start of the school year, and a handful of them would leave in 1899. The turnover resulted from the membership of the Board of Regents shifting toward a Populist majority in 1897 before Republicans regained a majority in 1899.

The 1899 Board of Regents canceled the scheduled commencement address of former presidential candidate William Jennings Bryan, known for his populist leanings. Willard remembered it "was quite generally condemned as bad taste, bad tact, and bad business for Manhattan."[4]

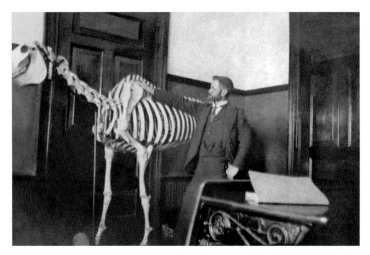

Charles W. Pape was the museum's assistant curator from 1897 to 1899 and is seen here in the spring of 1898 using a horse skeleton in instruction. An alumnus, Pape also was an assistant in veterinary science, zoology, and physiology.

It is a common misconception that "frontier" Americans were rough or unrefined. In actuality, the majority of nineteenth-century Americans took great pride in their personal appearance and grooming. Students Ernest M. Cook and Hiram A. Holzer were shown in a January 1899 scrapbook photograph that is humorously captioned: "Whisker Club."

Manhattan, Kansas, has a winter climate that can be very cold, but snow is not always common. Here students on the south side of Anderson Hall in about 1898 were taking time to enjoy some play in the snow. Because they are not wearing hats or winter coats, it is likely that this photo was staged.

KSAC women during the 1897–1898 school year included Daisy Hoffman and Julia Ehrsam.

When Mary Winston was elected chair of mathematics in 1897, she became the first woman on the KSAC faculty to hold a PhD. She had studied at the University of Wisconsin, Bryn Mawr College, and the University of Göttingen in Germany before arriving at KSAC. She left academia in 1900 to marry University of Kansas mathematics professor H. B. Newsom.

The Board of Regents replaced Will in 1899 with Ernest Reuben Nichols, a physics professor at Kansas State for nine years. Nichols, despite his reluctance to be president, was an efficient and hard-working administrator who successfully addressed the financial problems he inherited. He never ran a budget deficit and successfully lobbied for an almost tenfold increase in state funding. Over $400,000 went to the construction of nine buildings and the renovation of four more. New courses during Nichols's tenure included Animal Husbandry, Civil Engineering, and Printing. College extension services expanded to include a farmers' institute train. In 1901, the first branch experiment station began in Hays, with additional stations eventually developing in Garden City, Ogallah, and Dodge City. He also formed a council of deans to improve communication among administration, faculty, and students. Although Nichols raised admission and graduation requirements, student enrollment doubled beyond 2,300 by 1909.

Campus culture evolved during Nichols's administration. Literary societies, campus fixtures since the 1860s, maintained their prominence during the early twentieth century by holding regular meetings, recitations, and performances. Additional student groups developed, using Greek letters to announce their presence—many later became chapters of national organizations. Recreational and intercollegiate athletics also became more connected to the student experience. Baseball and football received a majority of the attention, but basketball and track gained interest. One of Nichols's last presidential efforts was the creation of a student council that continues today as Kansas State's Student Governing Association.

Prices at the college bookstore were fixed at cost plus expenses, leaving no profit margin. The dining hall hosted ten-cent lunches or twelve for $1.00 and twenty-one for $1.75. The printing office handled the *Students' Herald*, which previously had been outsourced to Manhattan printers.

Above Right: Ernest Rueben Nichols was KSAC's fifth president, from 1899 to 1909. His first year was on an interim basis, becoming the official president in 1900. He had been at KSAC since 1890, mainly as physics professor and head of the department. On his lapel in this photograph is a button with a picture of his wife, Marguerite Rae, and their young son, Rae. Nichols resigned the presidency in 1909 to manage a Chicago business called Thurston Teachers Agency.

Right: Mike Ahearn first coached the men's basketball team during the 1906–1907 season. They won five games and lost six, with one victory being a 29-25 win over the University of Kansas. Charles Melick had coached the inaugural KSAC men's basketball team the year before.

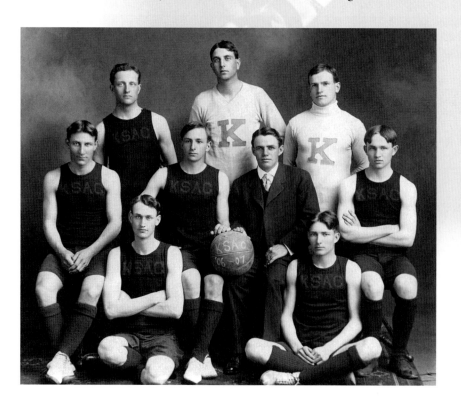

President Nichols had a humorous interaction after administering discipline to a group of pranksters. Fellow classmates told the president that the entire class would leave the college in protest, and Nichols replied, "Well, as far as I know the trains are running on time." The class remained.[5]

Nichols faced controversies that included funding agricultural education and protecting engineering education. One incident involved a vocal regent who sought greater budget allocations for agricultural work, even though Nichols had funded the department at higher levels than his predecessors. Eventually the regent resigned, but members of the media continued to press the issue throughout Nichols's presidency.

Another dispute involved Kansas State's engineering curriculum, which had existed for less than a decade and was quite popular. Some Kansas legislators, influenced by education lobbyists, proposed a bill that the University of Kansas should be the only school providing engineering education. Kansas State students responded by inviting legislators and others to visit campus and form their own opinions. In February 1909, about three hundred people arrived and enjoyed tours of campus, a program in the auditorium, and a three-course meal prepared by domestic science students. By the end of their visit many legislators, impressed with the scope and intensity campus activities, pledged to vote down the proposed bill.

After a state legislator introduced a bill to combine all engineering curriculum at the University of Kansas, KSAC students took action. About three hundred legislators, editors, and their spouses arrived on campus on February 3, 1909, in response to the students' invitation. Their visit included touring the college, attending classes, viewing a program of entertainment in the auditorium (seen above), and dining on food prepared by the domestic science students.

Students gathered in front of (and on) Anderson Hall
in about 1900 for this photograph. Many features of
Anderson Hall, such as porches and chimneys, have been
removed out of necessity or modernization. On the ground,
women are mostly on the left of the main entrance and
men are mostly on the right of it.

This spectator photograph shows Theodore Roosevelt, twenty-sixth president of the United States, visiting Manhattan on his 1903 "whistle stop" tour. He arrived on May 2 to a large crowd of students and community members, remaining for about fifteen minutes and speaking briefly about college life. According to the *Students' Herald*, the president advised students, "Play hard while you play; and when you work, don't play at all."

In about 1900 a carpentry class posed in front of the Shops building. Several of the men were wearing ribbons on their coats and vests, which may have been from a campus competition.

Students and instructors in a woodworking class, circa 1900, in the Shops building. Although these students were using hand tools, modern machinery powered by electric motors, such as lathes, can be seen in the background.

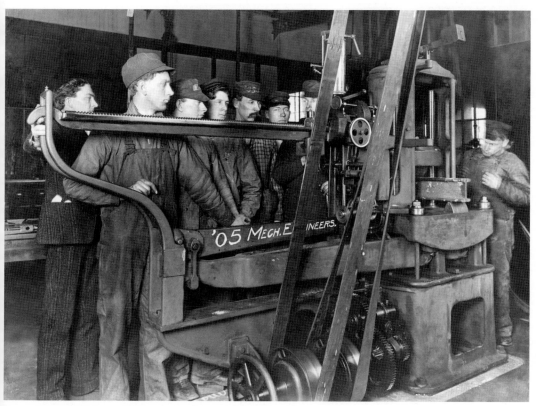

Mechanical engineering students and department head Edmund B. McCormick (on far left) were examining a Riehle Testing Machine in 1905. Their coursework mixed theory and practice, ensuring graduates had the requisite technical skills for engineering operations. The machine applied increasing loads to gauge the strength of various building materials. In this photograph, a steel beam was being tested.

Students—mostly likely from the Franklin Literary Society—posed in an offensive football formation on an unidentified Manhattan street, as well as in a more formal portrait on a sidewalk. In football's infancy, KSAC faculty considered it a distraction to students, although by the time of these photos the college had a team.

FOOTBALL SQUAD

Charles A. Groves was the first African-American athlete at KSAC. He is seen here in the 1903 football team photo (third row, center). Groves studied agriculture, writing his senior thesis on "Damage Sustained by Agricultural Lands in Wyandotte County from the Flood of 1903." (*Sunrise*, 1904 yearbook)

Members of the 1905 track and field team, like most of the college's athletes, came mainly from rural areas. The 1905 yearbook, *The Bell Clapper*, lamented that "although the farm is one of the best places for the development of the physical man, it fails to develop him in the quickness and alertness of mind and body that are essential to modern athletics." Charles W. Melick, assistant in dairy husbandry, coached track in 1905 and 1906.

The Alpha Beta Literary Society, seen here in costume, performed the play *East Lynne* in 1904. Other activities included writing poetry and short stories for their newspaper and yearbooks and providing an annual exhibition. Including men and women was integral to this society, as noted in the 1904 yearbook, *Sunrise*: "Co-education means much to the Alpha Betas, for they know that, sometime in life, men and women must work together; and, to obtain the best results, they should help each other now."

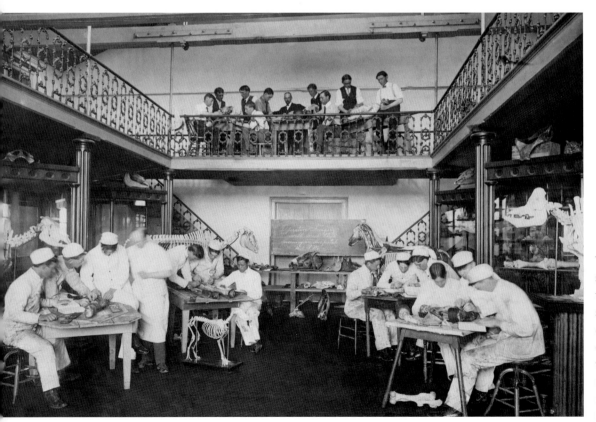

This 1907 view of the anatomy lab shows students working on one of the foundational courses in the veterinary science curriculum. The 1906–1907 catalog stated, "To emphasize the relation of the various structures of the body, and to note particularly the positions of organs most subject to surgical operations, the major part of the course is devoted to laboratory work."

ALMA MATER
Kansas State College
of Agriculture and Applied Science

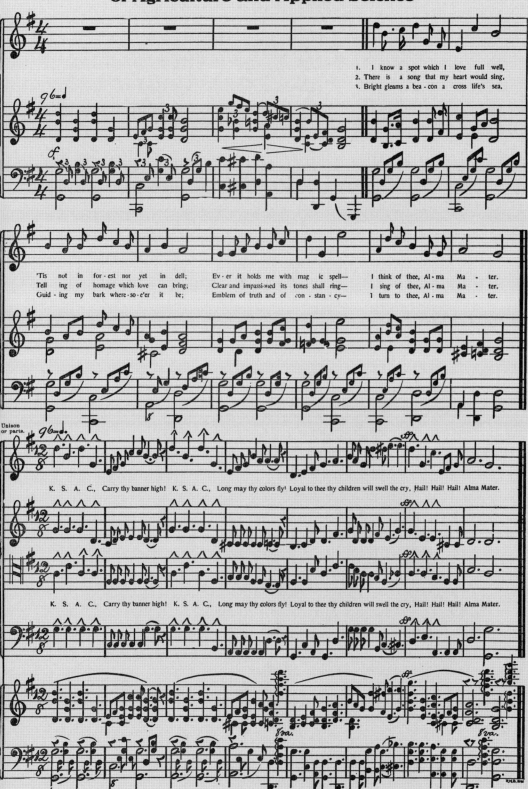

Humphrey W. Jones (Class of 1888) won a $25 prize for composing KSAC's official school song, *Alma Mater*, as part of a 1903 contest. The college's Bluemont Quartet gave the first public performance of the song a few months later at commencement ceremonies.

The KSAC battalion drilled in front of many onlookers on the lawn east of the Auditorium in about 1905. To the right is the cadet band. In that year, the U.S. government supplied the college with 395 cadet rifles, two three-inch ordnance rifles and carriages, as well as swords, target supplies, and ball and blank cartridges.

KSAC cadet John Porter is shown here in the attire male students were required to purchase for military training. The uniforms conformed to the West Point cadet pattern. The cap has the college emblem and the collar has K.S.A.C. in gilt metal letters. The 1906–1907 catalog suggested the uniform "makes a good serviceable suite for regular College wear."

Holtz Hall—known at the time as the Chemical Laboratory—was the scene of a fire on
May 31, 1900, that nearly destroyed the building. A student developing photographs in the
darkroom accidentally started the fire, which swiftly reached the attic. Student L. V. White
spotted it and sounded the alarm. After the fire, experts determined the exterior walls were
sound and renovated the structure to become a women's gymnasium based on the plans of
architecture professor J. D. Walters.

This undated photograph shows a KSAC forestry class in the field, likely
on a nearby private farm or within the college arboretum. Although
Kansas is not known as a land of trees, various species were widely
introduced during the last half of the nineteenth century. Further, the
Kansas Forest Service began in 1887, although it was 1909 before the
state attached it to KSAC and based it in Manhattan.

Domestic Science Club members attend a Japanese-themed evening party on November 10, 1904. The club began in 1876 with the purpose of assisting domestic science education at KSAC and membership included, among others, wives of faculty and community members.

Florence Ball directed women's physical fitness at KSAC from 1899 until her death from malaria in 1900. *The Industrialist* described her as a "pleasant, warm-hearted young woman of exemplary character" who was "loved and respected alike by collaborators and pupils." Physical fitness at the time was required of all freshmen and sophomore women, and activities included exercises that could be done any time, as well as more rigorous gymnastics. The basement of Fairchild Hall was where women exercised during this time.

Two female students playfully tease a male student inside one of the college's greenhouses next to Horticulture Hall. Candid scenes such as this one are rare and offer valuable glimpses into students' daily lives outside of the classroom.

A group of women from about 1900 gathered for this formal photograph on campus. Minnie Howell, the first female African-American graduate of KSAC, is likely to be standing at the far left. Howell was an active member of the Ionian Literary Society, played piano solos, and graduated in domestic science with a senior thesis titled "Healthful Homes." For about the next forty years she was involved in education, eventually becoming the head of home economics at Southern University. She returned to Manhattan toward the end of her life and directed the Douglass Community Center before her death in 1948.

This drawing depicts the KSAC campus in about 1905. The buildings from left include: Auditorium, Fairchild Hall, Kedzie Hall, Anderson Hall, Holtz Hall, Denison Hall (first one built in 1902), Holton Hall, Dairy Hall, and Horticultural Barn. The buildings in the upper right include: Shops, Horticulture Hall and Greenhouses, Agricultural Experiment Station, Armory, and Barns.

This panorama from about 1907 shows, left to right: Agriculture Hall (present-day Holton Hall), Dairy Hall (razed in 1994), and the newly finished Horticulture Hall (present-day Dickens Hall). Horticulture Hall was named for Albert Dickens (shown at left) in 1931. Dickens was graduated from KSAC in 1893 and 1901 and was in the horticulture department from 1899 until his death in 1930. He chaired the department from 1901 to 1930 and was the first state forester from 1909 to 1910. Dickens's cheery personality and devotion also helped build a strong alumni association.

The room of this student, likely Laurenz "Rennie" Greene, included a creative way to display prized photographs and possessions. The 1906 yearbook, *The Banner*, said he was "a favorite with everyone in general, the girls in particular." The academic efforts of this 1906 graduate included a senior thesis titled "Growing Conifers from the Seed."

Despite these successes, the Board of Regents had asked Nichols for his resignation more than a year earlier, citing directional differences. In 1909, they replaced him with Henry J. Waters, dean of agriculture at the University of Missouri. Waters's presidency was filled with much progress amidst the growing international unrest that resulted in World War I.

President Waters delegated many administrative responsibilities to deans and department heads, signaling Kansas State's growing complexity. In 1912, the Board of Regents reorganized courses of study into divisions—Agriculture, General Science, Mechanic Arts, Home Economics, and Extension. The next year, an administrative shift occurred when a statewide educational Board of Administration replaced the college's Board of Regents. At the same time, Waters implemented higher admission standards, requiring more high school credits from incoming students and necessitating an overhaul of coursework.

Higher admission standards also allowed national fraternities to sponsor chapters at Kansas State. Sigma Alpha Epsilon established the first fraternity in 1913 and Pi Beta Phi started the first sorority two years later. In 1917, African-American fraternity Phi Beta Sigma made Kansas State the site of its first chapter on an integrated campus west of the Mississippi River.

Above: Henry J. Waters served from 1909 to 1917 as KSAC's sixth president. After a successful tenure, he left to become editor of the *Kansas City Star*. During his time at KSAC, he was also president of the Kansas State Teachers' Association, president of the International Dry Farming Congress, special commissioner to the Philippines, and president of American Society for the Promotion of Agricultural Science. In addition, he authored five books during his life: *Essentials of Agriculture, The Development of the Philippines, Agricultural Laboratory Exercises and Home Projects, Essentials of the New Agriculture,* and *Animal Husbandry.*

Right: Some of the Sigma Phi Delta men gathered at midday in front of their house for this photograph in 1917. Fraternities, sororities, and honoraries have been an important part of KSAC student life for more than a century.

Athletics grew in popularity among students, faculty, and administration. In 1911, the completion of Nichols Gymnasium, the organization of an athletic council, and the building of on-campus athletic fields highlighted a new era for the college. These achievements allowed more students to participate in athletics and watch sporting events. During this time, Kansas State transferred membership to the Missouri Valley Intercollegiate Athletic Association.

Margaret "Marg" King was an active KSAC student with memberships in Ionian Literary Society, YWCA, the Prix, Zeta Kappa Psi, Omicron Nu, and Chi Omega. Seen here ready for some basketball, King was a 1918 home economics graduate.

Women were not permitted to play intercollegiate games during this era, so classes played each other and faculty. The 1910 *Royal Purple* reported the senior basketball team (shown here) received "beautiful black sweaters with bright '10s on them" from classmates in appreciation of "their hard work and pluck." The juniors won the 1910 championship.

The women's gymnasium (present-day Holtz Hall) around 1909 had a large drill hall (shown here), a dressing room with 150 lockers, an apparatus room, a lecture room, two small offices, eight showers, two tub baths, and four water closets. The building served as a gym until Nichols Hall was completed in 1911. This photograph shows an exhibit of corn in the west wing of the building.

Above: This image shows the crowning of the 1910 May Day Festival queen, Rena Faubion. M. S. Collins was the master of ceremonies for this event that included musical performances, cultural dances, foot races, and baseball games. The *Students' Herald* reported that "the most beautiful [event] was the winding of the May Pole" as twenty-four women—dressed in white and carrying KSAC pennants—danced and circled the pole. The paper further noted three thousand attendees enjoyed the inaugural event, which became an annual affair until 1929.

Above Left: Student Gladys Nichols used these tickets in 1910 to attend baseball games and the inaugural May Festival. The baseball team amassed a 17-3 record, with F. P. Parks as captain and centerfielder and Mike Ahearn as coach. The YMCA and YWCA teamed with the Women's Athletic Association to sponsor the May Festival.

Below: The KSAC baseball team is seen here in about 1910 playing an unknown opponent on the field located at the site of present-day Bluemont Elementary School. After Nichols Gymnasium opened in 1911, the baseball team had indoor practice space and the team moved to the new Alumni Field next to campus.

This 1914 football game was played on KSAC's athletic field that ran east and west about where the Alumni Center is today. Guy Lowman was the head of physical education from 1911 to 1915 and coached every sport but track. His final year coaching football was 1914, and Merrill "Red" Agnew captained the team to a 1-5-1 record.

Harvey Roots and Jack Gingery, senior tackles on the 1909 team, played football under Mike Ahearn. Gingery was captain of a 7-2 team that lost the two games by a total of five points (3-0 and 5-3) and outscored everyone else 317-3.

A mad scramble for the football occurred during this early version of the Sunflower Showdown. KSAC (in striped sleeves) battled the University of Kansas on the athletic field where the Alumni Center is today. Buildings in the background include Calvin Hall, Kedzie Hall, and Anderson Hall. The undated photo likely is from 1915 or 1917, both of which the Jayhawks won.

1909-1910
MEMBERSHIP CARD

1909-1910
MEMBERSHIP CARD
THIS CERTIFIES THAT
M *Gladys Nichols*
IS A MEMBER OF
K. S. A. C. ROOTERS' CLUB
Carrie McGott, PRESIDENT
Nell M. Hickok, TREASURER

Gladys Nichols had this 1909–1910 Rooters' Club membership card. A few male students had organized the club in 1905 to attend KSAC football games and financially support the team. The main responsibility of the Rooters' was to visit opposing teams to establish sportsmanship and a spirit of fairness. During games, Rooters' would wear college apparel and regalia to show their loyalty. In 1906, female students organized a women's Rooters' Club to work with the men's group. Prior to football games, the women would march slowly around the outside of the field, waving a large KSAC banner while following Boscoe, a large black dog wearing the colors of the college.

Construction on Nichols Gymnasium began in 1910, addressing growing athletics and military drilling needs. One of the first buildings in the U.S. to have a continuously poured concrete floor, Nichols Gymnasium housed two swimming pools and a basketball court. Named after President Ernest R. Nichols, it was home to departments such as women's physical education, military science, and music.

Far Left: Raymond "Shrimp" Adams was an animal husbandry major who captained the men's basketball team in 1916. The *Royal Purple* reported he and teammate Frank Reynolds were "easily the best pair of forwards in the Missouri Valley." They and Earl "Slim" Ramsey were chosen for the All-Missouri Valley team that year.

Left: Herbert H. Frizzell ran track for KSAC from 1914 to 1916, setting a high jump record his first year that lasted decades. When the "Oklahoma Kangaroo," as his teammates called him, did not compete, he studied animal husbandry, graduating in 1916.

On December 7, 1916, President Waters (holding shovel at left) led students, faculty, and citizens in a field day to improve conditions on the athletic field. Classes were canceled and 1,200 people started the work of leveling the field, improving drainage, and providing food and drinks. By the end of the day 2,500 people had helped, and Julius T. Willard remarked, "Nothing else equal to it has ever been put on at the College."

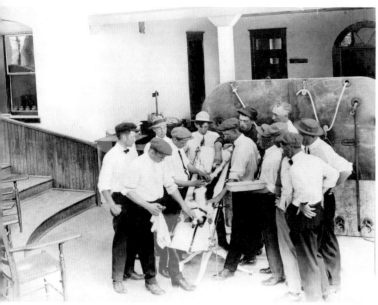

Veterinary science students can be seen honing their skills on a dog in Leasure Hall in 1915. In 1908, KSAC received state funding to construct this building for veterinary science and the department of bacteriology.

Waters also significantly expanded extension programs by creating the Division of College Extension. With federal support through the Smith-Lever Act of 1914, extension work at Kansas State included farmers' institutes (later called Farm and Home Week), agricultural trains, farm bureaus, 4-H, extension schools, and a home study department. In addition, new experiment stations in Colby and Tribune, as well as the creation of the engineering experiment station, provided more research opportunities to faculty and students.

Those researching agricultural subjects at Kansas State had explored animals, insects, plants, and soils, discovering solutions that included the blackleg vaccine and the hog-cholera serum. Others studying engineering topics had investigated road and building construction, making advances with concrete, electrical transfer properties, heating methods, and power-plant economics.

KSAC often promoted its agricultural and mechanical focus by profiling various farm implements, such as this Case Model 10-20 tractor built between 1915 and 1918 on which a woman is seated.

As part of KSAC's extension services, an agent is seen here giving a spraying demonstration at Mr. D. W. Layer's orchard in about 1916. Pest control was a crucial component of improving harvesting yields and was part of KSAC's agricultural curriculum.

A poultry husbandry class is shown working outside in this undated photograph. William Lippincott, with KSAC from 1912 to 1923, was the first professor of poultry husbandry. The 1915-1916 catalog, about the time of this image, gave this description of the Beginning Poultry course: "This course takes up a discussion of the various operations that go to make up the art of poultry keeping…. The laboratory study includes work in dressing, packing, and caponizing."

Part of KSAC's agricultural research and extension efforts included participating in public farm celebrations at the Fort Hays branch experiment station. One popular example was Roundup, seen in this image from 1917. Started in 1914, Roundup remains an annual event. Another was Sorghum Day, in which participants—including those from 1917 seen below—learned the value of using sorghum in their agricultural endeavors.

On October 28, 1911, visitors, faculty, and students attended the dedication ceremony and the unveiling of the William A. Harris bust. The former U.S. senator from Kansas was a member of the KSAC Board of Regents when he died in 1909. The bronze bust is located in front of Fairchild Hall.

This undated photograph shows a rope laboratory class on the north side of the Armory learning skills related to rope making.

The college battalion was in a firing line on the lawn in front of Anderson Hall in about 1916. Within a couple of years, these training sessions became part of KSAC's wartime transition.

In 1917, shortly after the American entry to World War I, President Waters resigned unexpectedly. He was involved in many outside activities—including war efforts—and felt his contributions to the college were complete. By then, Kansas State had graduated nearly 3,500 students since its founding in 1863, and Willard wrote that the college was "unquestionably one of the greatest in the [land-grant] system, and in some features unequalled by any other."[6]

— Cliff Hight

For further reading beyond the sources in the notes, see the following:

Carey, James C. *Kansas State University: The Quest for Identity*. Lawrence, KS: The Regents Press of Kansas, 1977.

Gelber, Scott M. *The University and the People: Envisioning American Higher Education in an Era of Populist Protest*. Madison, WI: University of Wisconsin Press, 2011.

Gibson, Virginia Noah. "The Effect of the Populist Movement on Kansas State Agricultural College." Master's thesis, Kansas State College of Agriculture and Applied Science, 1932. Available online at http://archive.org/details/effectofpopulist00gibs.

Kansas Quarterly 1, no. 4 (Fall 1969), Homer Socolofsky, editor. The issue was devoted to populism in Kansas.

1. Walters, *History of Kansas State Agricultural College*, 115.
2. Willard, *History of Kansas State College of Agriculture and Applied Science*, 119.
3. Mamie Alexander Boyd, *Rode a Heifer Calf through College* (Brooklyn, NY: Pageant-Poseidon Ltd., 1972), 95.
4. Willard, *History of Kansas State College of Agriculture and Applied Science*, 124.
5. Ibid., 170.
6. Willard in *A Standard History of Kansas and Kansans*, William E. Connelly, ed., vol. 2, 1035.

Floyd Wilson showed off his senior thesis, "Tests on a Smith Gas Producer," in this photograph taken in front the Shops building. He was a 1910 mechanical engineering graduate who also earned the rank of captain in the KSAC First Battalion.

In 1910, mechanic arts dean Edmund B. McCormick led efforts to establish the Engineering Experiment Station. The Board of Regents appointed McCormick, a faculty member from 1901 to 1913, as the station's first director. He oversaw experiments with building construction materials, concrete, heating methods and fuels, machinery fuels, and road construction materials during the station's infancy.

This was how KSAC's engineering building looked from the west in 1915. Today it is part of Seaton Complex.

Lithuanian immigrant and MIT graduate Andrey Potter was a member of the KSAC engineering faculty from 1905 to 1920, serving as dean and director of the Engineering Experiment Station for the last seven years. The KSAC agricultural engineering program he developed was among the first in the U.S. He left to become Purdue University's dean of engineering and played an important role in the direction of engineering education in the U.S. in the twentieth century, becoming known as "The Dean of Deans" of engineering universities.

Students were using the applied mechanics lab in 1914. Built in 1909 in Seaton Hall, the lab provided space for testing the strength of various materials using state-of-the-art equipment.

Civil engineering at KSAC was in its first decade when this photograph was taken in 1915. The concrete construction class poured a section of concrete in today's Seaton Court.

Professor J. C. Kendall, state dairy commissioner and animal husbandry department head, purchased this Buick electric truck (pictured next to present-day Holton Hall) in 1910. College creamery agents traveled to farms west and southwest of Manhattan to gather milk, eggs, and cream to supplement KSAC's unanticipated low supply of dairy products.

The Franklin Literary Society enjoyed their big social event of the year, the annual hayrack ride into the country, as shown here in about 1910. The college's big traction engine pulled the flat cars.

Above: An example of KSAC's extension efforts in practical training, this bed-making class was part of the six-month-long housekeepers' course. Directed toward young women unable to attend college, the 1909-1910 catalog stated "hundreds of girls who take this course each year go back to their homes with . . . knowledge and training which will enable them to meet their responsibilities."

Right: Women in the woodworking shop construct some type of frame, possibly as part of their home decoration course. A required class for home economics majors, the 1910-1911 catalog stated lectures taught "that the home should show that fine art and industrial art are not to be considered separately."

Below: Another example of student creativity is this July 1915 baseball game between items forged in the foundry. The frogs were in the field and the bootjacks were at bat, complete with baseball, bat, bases, scoreboard, bleachers, and fans.

KSAC student Jerome Chapman
climbed the one-hundred-foot-high
campus water tower in about 1915 to
take these two panoramic photographs
of campus, looking north and south.

In this undated photograph is an automobile parade, which students organized to celebrate special occasions or make social outings more festive.

The men's Webster Literary Society and the women's Eurodelphian Literary Society frequently interacted socially. In 1911, the two groups chartered a train for a memorable excursion to Wamego where they visited the city and its beautiful park.

KSAC celebrated its fiftieth anniversary in 1913 with activities that included this parade. Classes were canceled for three days: Students' Day, Alumni Day, and National Day. Additional activities included speeches, reunions, a luncheon, a military drill, and a reception. Julius Willard called it "an occasion of appraisal, congratulation, and promise."

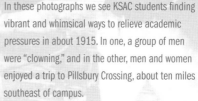

In these photographs we see KSAC students finding vibrant and whimsical ways to relieve academic pressures in about 1915. In one, a group of men were "clowning," and in the other, men and women enjoyed a trip to Pillsbury Crossing, about ten miles southeast of campus.

Above: At least four students were relaxing next to Wildcat Creek in about 1916.

Above Right: Fred "Red" Beaudette found a place on campus to sit in about 1917—the drinking fountain that was the gift of the Class of 1908. It originally stood in the quadrangle of Calvin Hall, Fairchild Hall, the Auditorium, and Nichols Gymnasium. After vandals destroyed the fountain in 1943, the class replaced it with a sundial in 1953, and it was moved to its present location in the Quad in the early 1990s.

KSAC extension services also supported community activities, as these photographs from about 1916 show. The volleyball game was played in Macon Township, Harvey County, about 110 miles southwest of campus. The sack race was part of the Sedgwick Township School Fair, in the township just south of Macon Township.

Inclement weather has long been part of campus life. Here, a spring hailstorm in 1915 caused over $1,000 worth of damage to the college's greenhouses.

A new agricultural building arose in 1913 as the Division of Agriculture outgrew its previous structure, today's Holton Hall. The new edifice, named Waters Hall in 1919, initially housed the Agricultural Experiment Station, a flour mill, and grain judging laboratories, as well as the departments of agronomy, animal husbandry, milling industry, and poultry husbandry.

→ Chapter 3 ←
Hardship and Opportunity,
1918–1943

The ROTC, organized on campus in January 1918, exercised on the athletic field in 1921. During World War I, it was suspended at KSAC until it was reorganized in 1919. Seaton Hall and the water tower are visible in the background.

William Jardine began his presidency at Kansas State in 1918 as the nation was mired in World War I and an influenza pandemic was emerging. After effectively leading the campus community through these initial hardships, Jardine focused the remainder of this tenure on expanding teaching, research, and service opportunities.

World War I caused significant short-lived changes on campus during President Jardine's first year. Instructional priorities shifted to emergency preparedness, improved food production, and enhanced war-related mechanical skills. For example, Kansas State's Reserve Officers' Training Corps (ROTC) unit became operational in January 1918 and the college's Students' Army Training Corps (SATC), a group of soldiers who studied specific subjects to improve their wartime contributions, began later that year. Also, toward the end of 1918 the campus community endured the influenza epidemic, causing five weeks of class cancellations and a three-month postponement of Jardine's inauguration.

As part of Kansas State's recovery from the Great War and influenza, Jardine's administration focused on quality teaching and added majors in business administration, chemical engineering, landscape architecture, music, nursing, and physical education. And in 1919, the administration split veterinary medicine from the Division of Agriculture to form its own division.

William Jardine arrived at KSAC in 1910 with an education and experience steeped in agriculture and the American West. A college-educated cowboy, Jardine understood theoretical and practical agriculture. After nearly three years as KSAC's agronomy professor, he became dean of agriculture and director of the Agricultural Experiment Station until he was selected as KSAC's seventh president in 1918. His understanding of agrarian success helped him guide the college through a very transformative time. Additionally, in 1923 Jardine and his family (wife Effie and three children) were the first to occupy the president's house on Wilson Court. After seven fruitful years at the helm, Jardine left in 1925 to become the secretary of agriculture for U.S. President Calvin Coolidge.

"Many changes have taken place here since I was a freshman. The institution has grown and the equipment has been improved a great deal but the students that come to us these days are not as serious minded nor as deeply interested in the practical side of agriculture as they used to be and one of our most difficult problems is the one of bringing them down to earth and getting them to realize that farming and livestock raising is not a silk shirt job. But after all, they are a bunch of well meaning boys, better trained in academic stuff than we were and they may come out all right in the end." Charles W. McCampbell, Kansas State alumnus and head of its animal husbandry department from 1918 to 1944, shared these impressions of the college's evolution when he wrote to a former classmate in 1924. [1]

Regimental bands from Camp Funston in Fort Riley performed at KSAC on Easter Day 1918. About three hundred instrumentalists gave this free concert outside the Auditorium after a recital by renowned baritone Oscar Seagle.

The Students' Army Training Corps (SATC), a group of soldiers who studied specific subjects to improve their wartime contributions, stood in formation in front of the Auditorium in 1918. Throughout the war, KSAC provided training space and education to these students. Earlier in 1918, KSAC had organized another student military group, the Reserve Officers' Training Corps, but suspended it for the duration of the war.

The SATC had training grounds on campus, and coeds at some point found them unoccupied. The women enjoyed a mock-training session.

Another academic unit that grew dramatically during this era was the Division of Home Economics. Mary Van Zile had served for over a decade as dean of women and dean of home economics when the administration separated the deanships in 1918. Van Zile continued supervising women's programs, while alumna Helen Thompson directed home economics. Thompson believed in pay equity and successfully worked for salary increases for women in her division. She also created the division's bureau of research, which studied topics that included child welfare, clothing and textiles, and human nutrition.

The first campus housing was Van Zile Hall, opening in 1926. Here is a view of early construction in which many local contractors promoted their connection with the project. Architecture department personnel worked with the state architect to design the building. It was named for Mary Van Zile, dean of women from 1908 to 1939 and dean of home economics from 1908 to 1918. Widowed at twenty-six, she raised two sons while finishing her education and serving in various educational capacities, including at KSAC.

Thompson Hall had facilities for home economics that included laboratories, instructional areas, a cafeteria, and a tearoom. Built in 1922, it was named for home economics dean Helen Bishop Thompson three years later. Thompson was a double alumna of KSAC who taught at various higher education institutions before returning to be dean from 1918 to 1923.

College extension opportunities expanded during Jardine's administration. World War I brought special focus on agricultural and home economics subjects addressing food conservation, effective use of farm products, and adapting to home life during war. After the war, demand for extension courses continued to grow. One innovative example of how Kansas State met these needs was the 1924 opening of the "College of the Air," an extension radio curriculum on home economics and crop and livestock production.

KSAC had a nursery school in Calvin Hall from 1927, the same year of this photograph, until 1940. It provided home economics students with opportunities to observe behavior and provide care for children in age from eighteen months to four years.

This undated photograph shows KSAC home extension agents holding a baby clinic as part of the state's better baby campaigns that started in 1915. These clinics enlisted women's clubs, doctors, nurses, civic leaders, and clergymen to promote healthy living and improved infant care. Often these events were held in conjunction with county and state fairs, and some of them included contests comparing babies' measurements with national weight, height, and health standards. Grade A, the same classification used to determine livestock quality, was the highest award for children—and parents—to receive.

Left: Additional extension work at KSAC included providing exhibits at numerous agricultural fairs, such as this one for the Kansas State Fair in 1924. Displays and demonstrations allowed extension personnel another way to accomplish the land-grant mission of sharing knowledge in agriculture, engineering, home economics, and other subjects.

Below: Beginning in May 1921, KSAC organized an annual agricultural fair with numerous events including shooting galleries, rodeo performances, dances, and a farmer's vaudeville. The student-led Agricultural Association oversaw the festivities, which in 1921 included over 3,500 attendees and ticket proceeds of more than $1,800. These fairs, according to animal husbandry department head C. W. McCampbell, helped teach students "organization and the value of teamwork, both of which are important factors in life."

A campus culture continued evolving with student exhibitions, social fraternities and sororities, and athletics. Students shared their academic efforts with the public through engineering open houses and agricultural fairs, which became annual events during Jardine's administration. Fraternities and sororities expanded and began overtaking literary societies as student social organizations. Intercollegiate athletics achieved greater popularity, and intramural athletics kept many students consistently connected to sports.

Horticulture professor Mike Ahearn became athletic director in 1920, a position he retained for twenty-six years. A man of varied interests, Ahearn designed much of the campus landscape early in his career, coached at least six sports, was a stickler for good grammar, and even decorated Nichols Gym for President Jardine's inaugural reception. Ahearn's perspective on athletics was this: "Be a good loser as well as a good winner—be a gentleman and scholar, both in the classroom and on the athletic field."[2]

This undated image shows KSAC athletic director Mike Ahearn (in golf attire) talking with University of Kansas athletic director Phog Allen (tipping his hat) in Memorial Stadium. Ahearn lettered in five sports while studying horticulture at Massachusetts Agricultural College (now University of Massachusetts Amherst). Often called the "Father of Kansas State Athletics," he actually came to KSAC as foreman of the greenhouses in 1904. While a horticulture instructor and professor, Ahearn coached football, basketball, baseball, track, tennis, and golf. In 1920, he became professor of physical education and director of athletics, which he held until 1946. He then attained emeritus status until his death in 1948. His successful teaching, coaching, and leadership elevated him to become one of the most respected figures in university history.

Jardine oversaw six construction projects, including a stadium built as a memorial to Kansas State students who died in World War I and other wars. The physical plant expansion—necessary to accommodate enrollment increasing 40 percent—was evidence of Jardine's ability to lobby for state funding and use it wisely. He also worked with private donors, combining their gifts with allocated monies to fund many of these construction projects.

President Jardine championed the effort to convert the athletic field into a stadium to honor the sacrifices of "soldiers who have fallen in battle and who were at one time students at this institution." The west side of Memorial Stadium, seen here, was completed in 1923 and the east side was finished the following year. Funding for the construction included a financial collaboration between college committees and community members.

This photograph was taken in 1925 on the day President Jardine left Manhattan to serve as secretary of agriculture for President Calvin Coolidge (1925–1929). Jardine's glowing reputation was evident as approximately 2,500 students, faculty, and community members wished him well. He went on to serve as U.S. ambassador to Egypt (1930–1933), Kansas state treasurer (1933–1934), and president of Wichita State University (1934–1949).

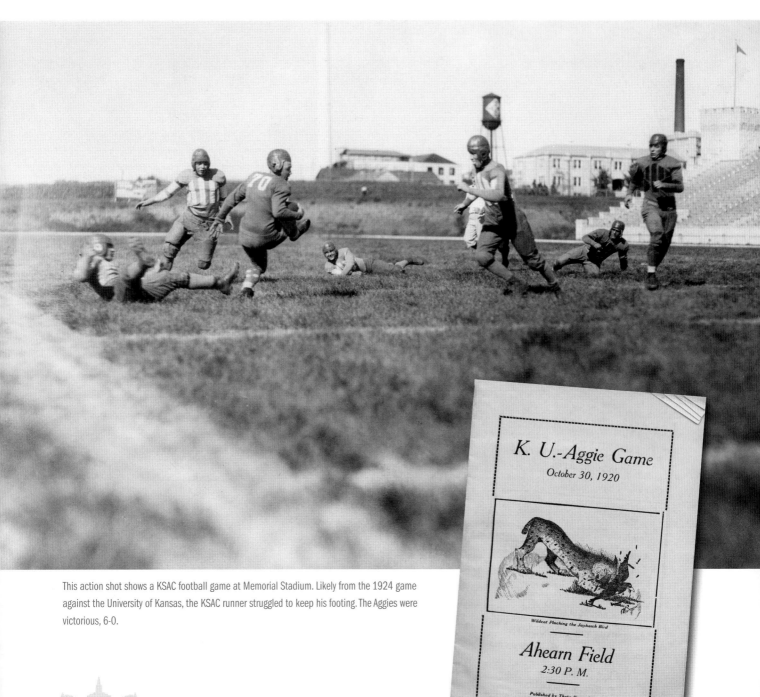

This action shot shows a KSAC football game at Memorial Stadium. Likely from the 1924 game against the University of Kansas, the KSAC runner struggled to keep his footing. The Aggies were victorious, 6-0.

K. U.-Aggie Game
October 30, 1920

Wildcat Plucking the Jayhawk Bird

Ahearn Field
2:30 P. M.

Published by Theta Sigma Phi
Women's Journalistic Fraternity

Right: Ray Watson, the first KSAC student to compete in the Olympics, participated in the 1920, 1924, and 1928 Games. Additionally, Watson won the 1921 NCAA Championship in the mile run—a first for the college. And he did all of this after overcoming a horrific shotgun accident as a teenager in which he lost his right hand. The 1921 *Royal Purple* praised the animal husbandry major as owning "a fleet pair of legs, a stout heart, and a world of endurance."

Left: Glenn Aikins played baseball at KSAC from 1922 to 1924 while completing his degree in agriculture. The 1924 *Royal Purple* noted he was a "brilliant fielder, a bad man with the stick, and an able leader." Aikins captained the baseball team in 1924 and successfully balanced his scholastic duties with athletic endeavors.

Below: Ivan Riley was the first KSAC athlete to medal in the Olympics. He earned a bronze medal in the 400-meter hurdles at the 1924 Olympics. The 1923 *Royal Purple* noted the architecture major "was the most outstanding athlete in the Missouri Valley in 1923" after winning multiple races and setting records—the U.S. record for the 440-yard low hurdles and world record for 40-yard high hurdles.

One of the most unique student-led traditions was Roughneck Day, which occurred annually from 1916 to 1924. A type of holiday usually associated with the Ides of March, Roughneck Day included a variety of strange, outlandish, and humorous attire and activities. These photographs are examples of costumes students wore during the event. Students also roamed Manhattan's streets holding unruly celebrations such as informal parades. There were various levels of support from the administration for the occasion until it became a day for students to skip classes and not participate. In early 1925, President Jardine announced KSAC was replacing Roughneck Day with an Easter vacation (which was the first spring break in college history).

"Among the Aggie traditions, the gayest was the Roughneck Day.... Crowds of students, as bare legged cavemen, painted fools, enticing cavewomen, ghosts, clowns, beasties, African princes, spooks and mandarins, howled and roved all over campus and the neighboring streets in delightful abandon, rounding off the day with a dance in the recreation center [in Anderson Hall], which was more like a subway jam."

Eugene Surmelian
"Kansas State Agricultural College," *College Humor*, page 119
September 1929

Automobile repair was one of KSAC's many subjects in mechanical arts. In this undated image, a student works on a car in the Shops building.

American food reporter Clementine Paddleford began her career writing for Manhattan's *Daily Chronicle* at age fifteen. A 1921 industrial journalism graduate of KSAC, Paddleford moved to New York City and was a food editor for newspapers such as *This Week*, the *New York Sun*, and the *New York Tribune*.

Established at KSAC in 1888, the Men's Glee Club is seen here in about 1920. Women's Glee Club started in 1891. Both organizations allowed students interested in choral activities to perform traditional and novelty pieces for a variety of audiences. Also known as Men's and Women's Choir, these groups remain a vibrant part of student life today.

Dean of Engineering Roy Seaton spoke at the 1921 dedication of the engineering building that later would bear his name. The expansion more than tripled the space available for engineering and architecture education. During his twenty-nine-year tenure as dean, Seaton drew plans for many campus buildings, enlarged the scope of engineering on campus, and served in World War I and World War II. He retired in 1954 after fifty years at KSC.

This display of students' woodworking projects, likely taken in the Shops building, highlights KSAC's efforts to continue offering courses in mechanical arts.

The Manhattan City & Interurban Railway Company started an electric trolley system in 1909 and extended a line to Anderson Avenue by the week of commencement. It was five years before a line entered campus at Seventeenth Street. Such transportation progress allowed students to live farther from campus at lower-priced rentals and spend five cents for a ride to classes. This option existed until the company changed to busses in 1928, after which they removed the tracks and switches from campus in 1931.

This 1922 Household Physics class tested a vacuum cleaner in Calvin Hall. Named for KSAC alumna and domestic science professor Henrietta Willard Calvin, the building accommodated home economics from 1908 to 1960 with space for instruction and testing some "domestic" technologies.

Engineering curriculum included forging classes in the blacksmith shop. These students gathered around a worktable in about 1921. The student on the left most likely is Poy Lim, one of a handful of Chinese students during that time.

One student wrote in a photo album of the 1921–1922 Wampus Cats, "They are all full of pep." It was a fitting assessment since they were the official KSAC pep organization from about 1920 until the 1960s. The group's main duties were to lead rallies at athletic events and organize multiple school-spirit activities throughout the year.

Music fraternity Phi Mu Alpha performed *The Mikado* in 1923. The *Industrialist* reported this production was a "thoroughly professional performance [that] was the result of months of labor."

Nelson Antrim Crawford taught English from 1910 to 1914 and was head of industrial journalism from 1914 to 1926. A prolific writer and editor, Crawford published ten works while at KSAC, including a stylebook for the American Association of Agricultural College Editors, two journalism textbooks, and multiple books of poetry. He took a one-year leave of absence in 1925 to serve as an assistant to U.S. Secretary of Agriculture William Jardine before resigning in 1926. He occasionally returned to campus, including teaching a writing course for a professor on sabbatical in 1952.

East Waters Hall and the judging pavilion (visible between the wings in this image) were built in 1913, followed by West Waters Hall in 1923. Named for President Waters, it has been the central agricultural building for one hundred years.

The president's home at 100 Wilson Court was completed in 1923 and has accommodated seven presidents. In 1912, the widow of former Manhattan resident Davies Wilson, Mehitable C. C. Wilson, bequeathed $20,000 to KSAC for whatever use the Board of Regents directed. By the time they took action, most of the construction costs were covered by the gift.

Above: In 1925, KSAC celebrated the fiftieth anniversary of home economics instruction on campus. This photograph includes Nellie Kedzie Jones, Abby Lindsey Marlatt, and visitors. Other jubilee guests included Henrietta Willard Calvin, Mary Pierce Van Zile, and a large number of alumnae. It was this occasion when President Farrell announced that three buildings would be named in honor of home economics leaders: Calvin Hall, Thompson Hall, and Van Zile Hall.

Below: This 1930 photograph of the meats laboratory in East Waters Hall is an example of opportunities KSAC offered students to learn practical agricultural education. Students here were learning about various cuts of pork.

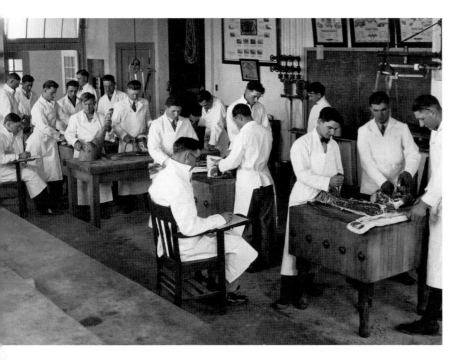

In 1925, after a fifteen-year tenure in roles that included agronomy professor, dean of agriculture, and president, Jardine left Kansas State to become the U.S. secretary of agriculture. Francis David Farrell, who had succeeded Jardine as dean of agriculture, became Kansas State's eighth president. His eighteen-year presidency included pockets of growth and progress despite economic instability and the effects of World War II.

Under Farrell's leadership, the Association of American Universities accredited the college in 1928. Curricula developed in subjects that included agricultural administration, home economics and journalism, and milling industry. Other instructional milestones during Farrell's administration included the celebration of fifty years of home economics education at Kansas State and the awarding of the college's first PhD (in 1933 to Hugh Stanley Carroll in chemistry). In 1935, the state legislature mandated military training for all men in their freshmen and sophomore years.

Farrell believed research at Kansas State should focus on traditional land-grant subjects like agriculture, engineering, and home economics. Agricultural research developed outside the experiment stations in fields throughout the state, either in cooperation with local farmers or on college lands. The breadth of research locations increased the local applicability of the findings for Kansas farmers.

Throughout the 1920s and 1930s, farm bureaus maintained a close relationship with Kansas State, providing another avenue of extension-type service. By 1940, more than one hundred county farm bureaus in Kansas had a combined membership of over eighty thousand. Associated with these bureaus were over 150 agricultural, home demonstration, and 4-H Club agents.

On campus, enrollment fluctuated as students and their families coped with hardships such as the Great Depression, severe drought, and the American involvement in World War II. One of the few bright spots was increased

President Farrell wrote that "the land-grant colleges are one of the most useful and influential features of the constantly increasing cooperation between the states and the Federal government in the development of the country and the safeguarding of our economic, social, and military welfare."[3]

Francis David Farrell succeeded Jardine as president of KSAC, after following him as a student at Utah State Agricultural College, employee at the U.S. Department of Agriculture, and dean of agriculture at KSAC. Highlights of his eighteen-year presidency from 1925 to 1943 included getting national accreditation for the college, changing the school's name to Kansas State College, and maintaining a faculty that reads like a list of campus buildings—including Ackert, Ahearn, Burt, Bushnell, Call, Cardwell, Dykstra, Holton, Holtz, Justin, King, Seaton, Throckmorton, Umberger, Van Zile, Weber, Weigel, and Willard. Unique among Kansas State presidents, Farrell and his wife, Mildred, were the only presidential family to have a baby while in office. Although he resigned in 1943, Farrell remained engaged academically on campus and was present when the library was named after him in 1955.

This undated photograph shows Mildred and Francis David Farrell seated beside the fireplace in the president's house. Above the mantel is Birger Sandzén's 1926 oil painting, *Still Water*. After Farrell's 1943 resignation, he spent the next two decades on campus studying and writing about rural Kansas agriculture and occasionally teaching agriculture and conservation courses.

admissions among graduate students. Nevertheless, budgetary constraints during the economic downturn resulted in declining salaries, a 13 percent reduction in faculty, and a general lack of funding for campus building projects.

Two significant administrative changes during Farrell's presidency included the 1925 establishment of the Board of Regents and the 1931 name change from Kansas State Agricultural College to Kansas State College of Agriculture and Applied Science. The Board of Regents replaced the Board of Administration that oversaw many state entities, and it became the main governing body for higher education in Kansas (and still is today). Farrell commented that the college's name change "simply means that the new name is more inclusive, more nearly descriptive than the old name was of what the College is and does and what it always has been and always has done."[4]

Farrell led the creation of a twenty-year plan in 1934 that focused on maintaining the college's land-grant mission, improving the quality of teaching and research, and adding liberal arts courses. These concepts largely aligned with Julius Willard's assessment at the time that Farrell "approves changes that bring progress, but he leans strongly toward conservation of that which has been found workable and productive of good results."[5]

American involvement in World War II deeply affected campus life. The military's Army Specialized Training Program (ASTP), like the SATC in World War I, had soldiers studying specific subjects, including engineering and veterinary medicine at Kansas State. Although the ASTP brought hundreds of temporary enrollees to campus, many others left Kansas State to join the military. Thus, enrollment for the 1942–1943 academic year, Farrell's final year as president, was the lowest in seven years and it would take four more years before admissions recovered.

Farrell retired as president in 1943 after leading Kansas State's wartime transition. He remained active on campus for two more decades, occasionally teaching agriculture and conservation courses while researching and writing about rural Kansas agriculture.

— Cliff Hight

For further reading beyond the sources in the notes, see the following:

Carey, James C. *Kansas State University: The Quest for Identity*. Lawrence, KS: The Regents Press of Kansas, 1977.

1. Charles W. McCampbell to Lyman J. Coffman, 29 February 1924, C. W. McCampbell Personal Correspondence, Animal Sciences and Industry records, Morse Department of Special Collections, Kansas State University Libraries.
2. "K-State Athletes Plan Memorial to Honor Ahearn," *The Kansas Industrialist*, 4 November 1948, 1.
3. F. D. Farrell, *"Prexy Says—": Comments on College Education and Related Topics* (n. p., n. d.), 7.
4. Kansas State College of Agriculture and Applied Science, *Biennial Report*, (Topeka, KS: Kansas State Printing Plant, 1932), 28.
5. Willard, *History of Kansas State College of Agriculture and Applied Science*, 404.

Known today as Historic Farrell Library, this was the first building on campus solely for a library. Constructed in 1927, it was named for President Farrell in 1955. Due to physical plant expansion during the 1920s, the administration in 1931 adjusted the time allowed between classes from five minutes to ten minutes so students could traverse a larger campus.

KSAC had a local Cosmopolitan Club for international students as early as 1913. In 1922, the local club, shown here in 1928, joined the national organization and continued to provide programs for students and faculty to better understand other cultures and nations.

The animal husbandry department started sponsoring a Sheep Day on campus in 1928 that included demonstrations and presentations of experiment results. This shearing demonstration was part of the 1930 Sheep Day.

The power plant building and 202-foot smokestack were built in 1928 and allowed KSAC to consolidate heat and power delivery in one building. It also marked time by a whistle blow at 8:00, 12:00, 1:00, and 5:00 each weekday for many years.

The "Lest We Forget" memorial, currently in General Richard B. Myers Hall, reminds viewers of the sacrifice students, faculty, and alumni made in World War I. More than 1,200 men connected to the college served. This black walnut display, originally placed in the recreation center in Anderson Hall, honors forty-eight who died during the war. One graduate student not on the list, Otto Maurer, joined the German army and died in Belgium during a battle with British forces.

The K Fraternity, seen here in 1929, started in 1913 to promote better athletics and to cooperate with the athletic department. Membership came with receiving a letter for intercollegiate athletics.

The 1931 KSAC baseball team, seen here, included Elden Auker, one of KSC's best all-around athletes (tallest, back row). He lettered in football, basketball, and baseball for three consecutive years and was a 1932 physical education graduate. Auker later pitched in the major leagues for ten years with the Detroit Tigers, Boston Red Sox, and St. Louis Browns.

Maintenance crews built three practice fields east of Memorial Stadium in early 1932, where the parking garage and K-State Student Union are today. On the right in this image is Seaton Hall.

KSC students played a game of pushball in Memorial Stadium as part of the eleventh annual Ag Fair on April 30, 1932. Pushball was a popular game in the early twentieth century in which each team had eleven players who attempted to push the ball under or over the horizontal bar of football goalposts for five or eight points, respectively. Because the six-foot-diameter ball weighed fifty pounds, injuries were common and hastened its demise as a sport.

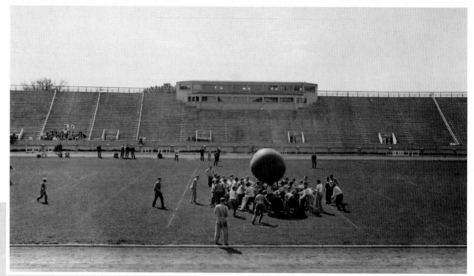

The Purple Pepsters, including these 1929 members, worked closely with the Wampus Cats to support athletics events. The Women's Athletic Association originally formed the pep organization in the early 1920s, and it later became the local representative of Phi Sigma Chi pep sorority. From formal rallies to attending national events, the Purple Pepsters encouraged a community of spirit and support for college sports until the 1960s.

The Alpha Delta Pi sorority gathered in front of their house at 518 Sunset Avenue for this photograph on a typical windy Kansas day in about 1933. KSC welcomed the original local chapter in 1914.

During the 1933 ROTC inspection, Colonel Richard McMaster posed with the honorary cadets (from left): Colleen Zacharias, Ethel Fairbanks, Adelaine Reid, and Ruth DeBaun. The annual event occurred in front of military officials and spectators that included KSC Vice President Julius Willard. The unit performed drills that included first aid, mass calisthenics, and rifle marksmanship. In 1933, the review occurred east of Thompson Hall near where the Beach Museum of Art is today.

This water pump was part of an old farmstead well located near Holton Hall. A gathering place for students and faculty to socialize, it provided water to campus until the installation of pipes in 1888. After decades of use, the pump was retired in 1937 when the well was filled. It was on display in Willard Hall for many years and today is in the university archives.

As part of the New Deal relief conglomerate in Kansas, the Federal Emergency Relief Administration (FERA), the Civil Works Administration (CWA), and a Riley County relief organization implemented a road improvement plan in spring 1934. One of these projects included the road east of Memorial Stadium, seen here on April 5. Other projects included paving a route west of Dickens Hall, removing the automobile park behind Waters Hall, and widening the Campus Creek road.

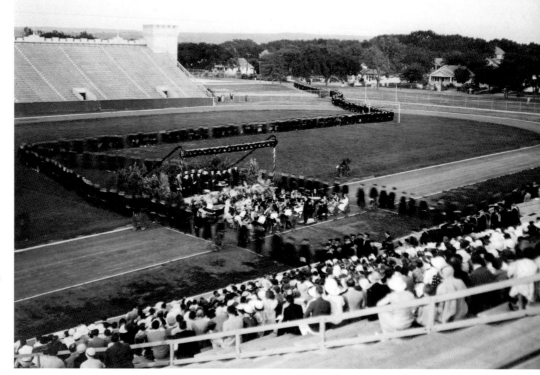

In 1934, the KSC administration moved commencement ceremonies from the Auditorium to Memorial Stadium to accommodate increased overall attendance and the growing number of new academic programs and degrees. This photograph shows graduates entering the southeast corner of the field to take their seats on the west side of the stadium.

Shortly after KSC's summer commencement in August 1934, fire consumed Denison Hall during the evening. The chemistry and physics departments lost significant research data (including seventy-five years of weather records), manuscripts, records, and equipment in the blaze. The chemicals in the building caused enough fireworks that onlookers compared the outburst to a volcano. A small vault saved some records, though.

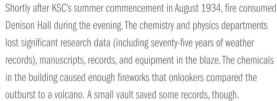

The 1934 football team became the first KSC team to win the Big Six Championship. Lynn Waldorf coached the team to a 7-2-1 record (5-0 conference) that included a tie with Manhattan (NY) College at Ebbets Field in Brooklyn. Those pictured here were the coaches and most of the twenty-four lettermen.

Above: KSC's engineering honor society, the Epsilon chapter of Sigma Tau, built this pyramid and dedicated it at the 1936 Engineering Open House. Originally located near the southwest corner of Seaton Hall, new inductees were required to paint the pyramid as part of their membership duties until the fraternity merged with Tau Beta Pi in 1974.

Right: Julius Willard took this photograph during a dust storm on March 20, 1935, from the north steps of Anderson Hall. The *Kansas Industrialist* reported that during the storm, bacteriology professor Arthur C. Fay performed an experiment with dust particles: "Calculations show that 34% of the dust particles inhaled were contaminated.... These figures are about a hundred times the normal count. Manhattan physicians attribute several cases of bronchial pneumonia to the dust laden air."

One of KSC's many student organizations included a chapter of the national honorary dancing organization Orchesis, which encouraged creative and aesthetic dancing for its female members. This photograph was from the 1936–1937 school year when Marjorie Forchemer was the faculty advisor. Women in this photo are (left to right): Avis Wynn, Garnetta Bell, Ruby Randall, Corrine Lancaster, Betty Lee McTaggart, Laura Jo Skillin, June Fleming, Sara Jane Antrim, and Jeanette Stearns.

One of many experiments conducted by the Agricultural Experiment Station included tests on concrete greenhouse benches. While simple in construction, studies showed these basic structures improved soil sterilization, encouraged better drainage, and reduced pest habitats. As a result, small crops and other greenhouse plants flourished.

KSC has a long tradition of successful livestock judging teams. This photo shows the 1936 international championship team looking over two young KSC bulls. The men are (left to right): Tom Potter, Alfred McMurtry, Wilton Thomas, Roy Freeland, Clare Porter, Clarence Bell, and Carl Elling.

Students protested in 1937 for funding to build a structure to replace Denison Hall. The journalism fraternity and sorority led the effort by depicting a camp and battle zone in the ruins and establishing a nearby "Red Cross Headquarters" to highlight the budgetary conflict. Bernice Scott, Willabeth Harris, Virginia Appleton, and Garnet Shehi (seen here, from left to right) joined others who dressed as nurses to promote their cause. The conditions in the ruins represented the political back-and-forth that slowed funding, and some students actually slept there some nights. Just over two weeks later, Governor Walter Huxman signed the appropriations bill that included $450,000 for the new science building.

Below: Thirteen months after the student protest for a new science building, Governor Huxman spoke to 2,500 people at the cornerstone dedication on April 20, 1938. Willard Hall, named for longtime KSC professor Julius Willard, was ready for use when classes started in September 1939.

KSC students made the best of what a January 1937 blizzard left behind. Called coasting at the time, the students went sledding in their cold-weather gear most likely on the lawn in front of Anderson Hall.

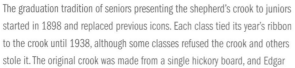

The graduation tradition of seniors presenting the shepherd's crook to juniors started in 1898 and replaced previous icons. Each class tied its year's ribbon to the crook until 1938, although some classes refused the crook and others stole it. The original crook was made from a single hickory board, and Edgar Dearborn and Bill Hopper made a brass crook in 1910 to replace the broken wooden one. In May 1938, Edgar Dearborn photographed both shepherd's crooks on the porch of his Manhattan home at 810 Poyntz Avenue. In one, Harriett Nichols Donohoo, Class of 1898, held a piece of the wooden crook with the brass crook behind her.

Archery instruction occurred in two women's physical education courses. This class from about 1938 practiced their technique south of Memorial Stadium, where the Alumni Center is today. Two years earlier, the *Royal Purple* reported that one archery class "hunted wild animals at the Rotary camp! The animals submitted to capture well—they were made of cardboard."

Between February and October 1938, KSC commemorated its seventy-fifth anniversary with many activities celebrating the growth and impact of the college. One event was a special parade that included historical displays of the college and agriculture that included community organizations and KSC. Psychology professor Roy Langford impersonated President Joseph Denison, as seen in front of the college. One of the floats, seen here along Poyntz Avenue, highlighted the agricultural progress of the college and the state.

Leon R. Quinlan served as KSC horticulture professor from 1927 to 1964, was the campus landscape designer from 1927 to 1951, and started the landscape gardening program in 1934. As professor emeritus, Quinlan was instrumental in starting the Kansas Landscape Arboretum on the western shore of Milford Lake in 1972. The university has honored his contributions in various ways as the campus has changed. Today, the Quinlan Visitor Center of the Kansas State University Gardens bears his name.

Margaret Justin, a 1909 alumna, was dean of home economics from 1923 to 1954 and continued with KSU for two more years. Her national reputation grew as she led the expansion of the program to include six departments, three home management houses, and a nursing school. She also authored or co-authored three books, each having multiple editions. Justin Hall, completed in 1960, was named for her. In connection with KSU's 1963 centennial celebrations, Justin was awarded the university's Distinguished Service Award.

KSC experiment station demonstration trains played an important role in advancing college curriculum and farm science throughout the state. Here, soils specialist W. H. Metzger demonstrates an analysis of Kaw Valley soil for Frances Casement as plant pathologist John O. Miller looks on. Clinics often accompanied informational cars in demonstration trains.

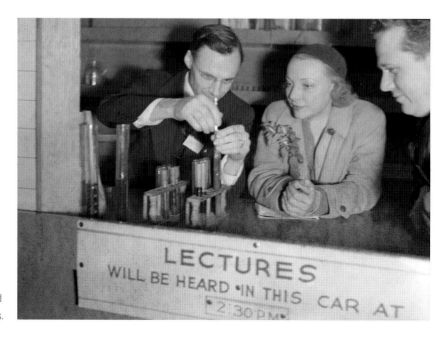

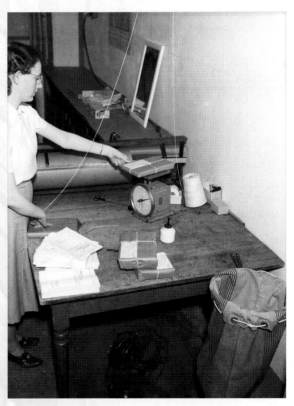

As part of KSC's extension services, clerks worked in Anderson Hall processing postal requests for bulletins. These photographs from May 1940 show Marie Brunker seated at her desk, retrieving bulletins from their files and working with other clerks to prepare mailings. Helen Litel is seen weighing packages before shipment. These activities were central to the publication and distribution of the college's key scientific studies and farmer recommendations.

This extension service photo was taken in October 1942 on the Orville Burtis ranch outside of Manhattan. The ranch became part of the Konza Prairie Biological Station.

Under the watchful eye of industrial journalism professor Edgar Amos, students in the 1941 typography laboratory worked at type cases in Kedzie Hall. The catalog that year described the course this way: "Typesetting, proofreading, correction of forms, as a background for journalism."

Left: This undated photograph, taken on the Earl Bunge farm in Coffey County, shows KSC extension crops specialist Eugene A. Cleavinger (right) sharing information about agricultural limestone properties with Albert Criger (center) and Louis C. Williams (left). Criger was chairman of Kansas's Agricultural Adjustment Administration (AAA) committee and Williams was KSC's assistant dean and assistant director of extension.

Below: This photograph shows the Kansas AAA committee meeting at the state office in Manhattan in 1942. From left to right: Albert Criger, Lawrence Norton, Emmet Womer, Herman Praeger, and Harry Umberger. Of note is the poster on the wall: "America has plenty of food for everyone." Umberger was a 1905 alumnus who returned to work for KSC from 1911 to 1912 and 1915 to 1947. Best known as dean of extension from 1919 to 1947, Umberger was heavily involved in sharing college research with the public through multiple forums. Umberger Hall was named for him upon completion in 1956 and is still home to K-State Research and Extension.

Chapter 4

Becoming a Modern University, 1943-1975

A post-World War II influx of students and veterans puts pressure on the college to provide housing. Former servicemen who were married lived in "Trailerville" (shown in 1946) located at the southeast corner of Claflin Road and Denison Avenue.

After eighteen years as president of the college, Francis D. Farrell, satisfied with how Kansas State had adjusted to the war effort, stepped down. The Board of Regents soon announced Milton S. Eisenhower as the ninth president. A native Kansan (born in Abilene in 1899) and Kansas State alumnus (Class of 1924), Eisenhower inherited a campus that needed to move beyond its agricultural and mechanical roots. He brought several strengths to the office including an understanding of the state, the college, agricultural issues, and international experience.

As summarized in his 1950 *Report to Kansas,* Eisenhower stated a college must have clear and obtainable goals for its educational programs. More specifically, for Kansas State to succeed, students had to acquire specialized training to make a livelihood, receive an understanding of the broad fields of knowledge, become proficient in the art of communication, obtain a capacity for making sound judgments, and gain an abiding commitment to the democratic way of life.

President Milton S. Eisenhower, First Lady Helen Eakin Eisenhower, Milton Jr., and Ruth pose for a family portrait on the steps of the president's campus residence on Wilson Court. Eisenhower was K-State's only native Kansan and alumnus to head the university. He was the younger brother of Dwight D. Eisenhower, president of the United States, 1953–1961.

A 1940s scene shows threshing in progress at K-State's first branch experiment station established in 1901 at Fort Hays. In 1945, there were four branch experiment stations conducting agricultural research under the direction of the central station located in Manhattan. Results were used extensively in class instruction.

Although Eisenhower appreciated that college programs needed to support wartime efforts, he proceeded with a plan to incorporate liberal educational goals for Kansas State. Faculty committees advanced new teaching methods to emphasize critical thinking, improve communication skills, instill social and civic responsibilities, and liberalize technical curriculums. Comprehensive courses for freshmen and sophomores emphasized social studies, biological and physical sciences, and humanities while juniors and seniors focused on subject areas of interest.

Eisenhower developed a number of undergraduate and graduate programs including veterinary medicine, physics, foods and nutrition, animal husbandry, and elementary education. Enhanced agricultural research led to important developments in crops, animal production, bakery science, and agricultural experiment stations. When Eisenhower departed, research funding more than doubled returning $100,000,000 to the state in earnings. Expanding academic programs coupled with dramatic increases in postwar enrollment (1941:4,108; 1944:1,300; 1948:7,000) resulted in a campus building boom.

Eisenhower also created an Institute of Citizenship that offered courses stressing the role of civic participation at the local, state, national, and international levels. Development of a UNESCO partnership with the state grew into one of the country's most active programs, reflecting Eisenhower's desire to increase international student enrollment.

Above Right: Dean R. I. Throckmorton conducts scientific research on wheat on the college agronomy farm north of campus, 1948. Throckmorton began working at K-State in 1911. He served as dean of the College of Agriculture from 1947 to 1951 and director of the Agricultural Experiment Station from 1946 to 1952. Throckmorton Hall was completed and named in his honor in 1981.

Right: The state legislature appropriated $92,500 in 1945 to purchase land, equipment, and livestock for the Grass Utilization and Pasture Management Project (shown in 1950). Experiments were conducted in Manhattan and Hayes.

Due to racial prejudice on campus and in the Manhattan community, Eisenhower took measures to address inequalities. Meetings with students, faculty, and community leaders, often behind the scenes, improved integrated student housing, businesses, and intramural programs. African Americans participating in varsity athletic programs received scholarships.

Increased financial resources for educational and resource programs as well as campus development resulted with the establishment of the Endowment Association in March 1944. Eisenhower worked with prominent citizens and legislators to hire additional faculty and increase salaries.

Similar to other universities, Kansas State confronted changes in higher education during the postwar period. Expanded curriculums, programs, and physical facilities reinforced Eisenhower's educational philosophy, which incorporated the liberal arts with traditional land-grant programs. His actions helped move the college to a modern university. Satisfied with his accomplishments, Eisenhower accepted the presidency of Pennsylvania State University in 1950, an institution that offered more opportunities to further advance his vision for higher education.

Delegations gather at the International Security Assembly in the old Auditorium, 1946. Organizations attending the student version of the United Nations chose countries to represent in discussions of world peace problems. Many delegates wore traditional clothing. About one thousand visitors, including high school students, observed the proceedings from the balcony. The event aligned with President Eisenhower's emphasis on internationalism. (RP)

Although part of the School of Engineering and Architecture's curriculum, students enrolled in the School of Arts and Sciences could take freehand drawing courses as electives (studio shown in 1944). The two-credit-hour course required six hours of laboratory work per week. (RP)

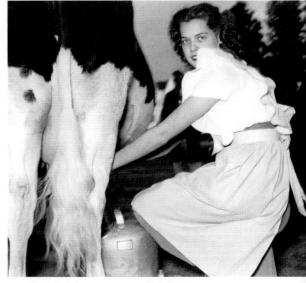

KSC's Ag Barnwarmer contest represented a longstanding campus tradition. Beginning in 1927, Ag Queen selection included a dance and farm performance review. Each contestant was rated by how she milked cows and other farm chores such as pitching hay, calling pigs, or operating tractors.

President Eisenhower attends the Little American Royal, 1950. Students competed annually for fitting and showing honors at the Livestock Pavilion between East and West Waters Halls. In 1951, the event moved to Ahearn Field House; three thousand people attended the show.

According to a 1951 article in the *Kansas State Collegian*, the Dairy Bar in Waters Hall was a place that students could go to find "ice cream and other cooling snacks..." and "served about a thousand students, faculty members, and college workers a day." In 1963, the Dairy Bar was relocated in Call Hall.

Built in 1911–1912, Dewey Ranch (shown in 1944) is now the headquarters for the Konza Prairie Biological Station, a field research station on the native tallgrass prairie preserve southwest of Manhattan. Operated by the K-State Division of Biology, the Konza is owned by Kansas State and the Nature Conservancy.

President Eisenhower and dignitaries gather at the Rock Springs Ranch dedication, 1946. 4-H members across the state raised $22,500 to buy the 348-acre tract of land south of Junction City for the State 4-H Club Camp. Rock Springs Ranch continues to be used for many KSC events and activities.

Over five hundred people listen to President Milton Eisenhower's dedication speech for Danforth Chapel on October 9, 1949. The World War II memorial was the first building on campus devoted solely to religious meditation and worship.

KSC plays a home baseball game (circa 1950s) at Griffith Park, located at the intersection of Fort Riley Boulevard and South Manhattan Avenue. Named after former first baseman and team captain Evan Griffith (Class of 1922), the stadium was home to the Wildcats until Frank Meyers Field opened in 1961.

"Sparky" served as a KSC mascot for one season making its appearance at a football game in 1947. Adrea Dee Simmons, a local high school student, played the role of the mascot. Willie the Wildcat didn't appear until 1964. (Alumni Association)

Left: Basketball fans in Nichols Gym make it clear the cramped and outdated facility needed replacement, circa 1940s. Their wishes came true with the construction of Ahearn Field House, the fifth largest field house in the nation when completed in 1951.

Below: Ahearn Field House, the future home court for KSC basketball, takes shape as Bennett Construction Company workers finish the flooring in 1950. Balcony seating accommodated 5,400 fans in stadium-type seats while the main floor seated 7,600.

President Milton S. Eisenhower (left) greets incoming president James A. McCain. The two shared a background in journalism, excelling as writers and public speakers, and the university's public image was of great concern to both.

In 1950, James A. McCain accepted the Board of Regents' offer to serve as K-State's next president. His twenty-five-year tenure included numerous changes in higher education that reflected a more liberal society and culture. Enrollment increased significantly during McCain's presidency. New students meant additional faculty, with many more holding doctorate degrees.

As the need for financial support increased, funds for research rose from approximately $1 million in 1950 to over $10 million after 1970—over two-thirds of the revenue came from government sources. Kansas State's programs supported the state's economy and by 1970, more than $200 million of annual farm income was attributable to the college's scientists and researchers. The placement of extension specialists and agricultural agents in all 105 counties enhanced the university's land-grant mission to serve the people of Kansas.

The physical plant reflected campus growth during the McCain era with construction or renovation of more than thirty buildings. Additional land, including the Konza Prairie Research Natural Area, was obtained for university use.

President James A. McCain and his administrative team, 1958. From left to right: Max Milbourn (assistant to the president), Dan Beatty (business manager), McCain, Herbert Wunderlich (dean of students), and A. L. Pugsley (dean of academic administration).

President James A. McCain and First Lady Janet McCain celebrate Christmas at Wilson Court with their daughter, Sheila, in 1955. As K-State's tenth president, McCain served from 1950 to 1975, longer than any president before or since. (RP)

When Faculty Senate was established, Rufus F. Cox became the first president elected to the office serving during the 1951–1952 academic year. He was head of the Department of Animal Husbandry, 1950–1966.

Students receive hands-on experience processing milk in the dairy facility located in West Waters Hall, circa 1951. The glass bottles are labeled with Kansas State College Dairy and the college seal. The dairy manufacturing curriculum prepared students to enter the dairy processing industry.

KSAC, the campus radio station, broadcasts jointly with Manhattan's KMAN to provide twenty-four-hour coverage during the 1951 flood. KMAN's station was inundated by floodwaters. The flooding devastated the Manhattan area, and the college provided shelter and provisions for many residents.

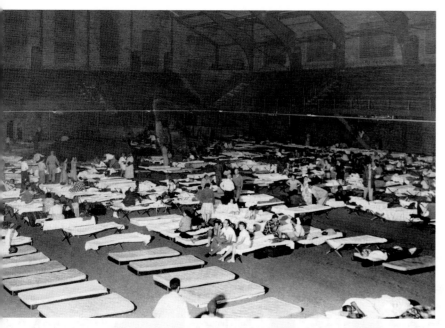

Cots set up in Ahearn Field House provide a safe haven for residents displaced by the 1951 flood. Many flood victims had been rescued from rooftops by a Coast Guard helicopter, which landed on the Memorial Stadium football field. East and West Stadium and Nichols Gym also sheltered victims.

Bagging flour gives a milling technology student practical experience, 1954. To obtain senior classification for this degree, majors must have worked for at least three months in a bakery, feed mill, flour mill, wheat elevator, or cereal chemistry laboratory. (RP)

30TH. ANNUAL 4H ROUND-UP.
MANHATTAN, KANSAS.   MAY 25-29, 1954.

Kansas 4-H members form a different shape every year for the annual commemorative Roundup photograph. In 1954, the Collegiate 4-H Club was the largest organization on campus with 350 members. They assisted with Roundup activities including recreation, guided tours, classes, and a trip to Rock Springs Ranch.

Students produce shows in a television laboratory for other classes to study and critique, 1955. The College of Arts and Sciences offered courses in television production, programming, advertising, writing, management, and dramatic techniques. Television laboratory courses were offered as early as 1948 for seniors and graduate students in electrical engineering. (RP)

Sergeant Charles Boerner instructs Air Force ROTC cadet James Hotchkiss on the use of the Link trainer in 1956, equipment used in training programs nationwide. The flight simulator, located in the military science building, was used to give cadets basic instruction on how to fly. (RP)

The Block and Bridle Club was the largest of its kind in the School of Agriculture. Its main goal was to promote animal husbandry in colleges and universities as well as contribute to the expansion of community involvement in agriculture. In 1957, members participate in a "frontier dance." (RP)

Food serving area in the K-State Union shortly after the original building was completed in 1956. Additions were finished in 1962 and 1970 and a renovation in 2000.

Students found themselves in Ahearn Field House to enroll in the fall of 1957. With increasing enrollment, this was the first time the field house was needed for the registration process. (RP)

Students walk along Manhattan Avenue to their residence hall after shopping at Aggieville's Campus Bookstore. The *Royal Purple* playfully suggested that a student's physique would also improve with each carry: "Strong arms are bound to result from carrying books to the dorm from Aggieville and later around campus." (RP)

Moving day for students in the 1950s, as it does today, often included the entire family. (RP)

The aftermath of the 1957 fire in East Waters Hall reveals the scope of damage. The early morning blaze started in the flour mill and rapidly destroyed the Departments of Flour Milling and Agronomy, as well as the meats laboratory in the Department of Animal Husbandry. Much irreplaceable research was lost.

Swimmers compete in Nichols Gym, circa 1957. The athletic department discontinued competitive swimming in 1968 due, in part, to an inadequate pool for practice. Even after Nichols Gym burned, the pool in the basement continued to be used for recreational purposes and swimming lessons until the natatorium opened in 1972.

Alice Venburg handles switchboard calls in the K-State telephone office, circa 1958. Operators were familiar with the campus and handled incoming long distance calls and those from Manhattan's telephone system. Before the college installed its own telephone exchange in 1947, calls came through the city's system and were costly.

An ad for the campus bookstore describes this scene, "A pair of firsts—a brand new student body witnesses the first pep rally of the 1958 season, preceding the first home football game against the University of Wyoming. K-State cheerleaders cavort before students attending the Aggieville Jamboree in September." (RP)

Associate Professor Murlin Hodgell and students work on a projected design for K-State's campus during a 1958 architecture class.

Students watch classmates wield torches as sparks fly in a 1958 welding class. The industrial technology curriculum in the School of Engineering and Architecture placed an emphasis on shop work and fabrication processes. (RP)

In 1956, KSC began an exchange program to provide technical assistance to educational institutions in India with support from the Agency for International Development. Over the years many faculty, technicians, and graduate students went to India to participate. Shown here in the early 1960s is a member of the K-State delegation assisting a group with threshing.

It became increasingly evident that Kansas State could not operate on funds appropriated by the state legislature (38 percent of total expenditures by 1970). To address this decline McCain established an endowment office with a full-time director and significantly increased scholarships and financial aid programs to support current and incoming students.

Like Eisenhower, McCain emphasized the importance of internationalism. Countries received technical assistance and opportunities for sharing cultures on a global context. Beginning in the mid-1950s, Kansas State established agricultural and veterinary programs in several countries including India and Nigeria as well as study abroad opportunities in Germany and Colombia. Various programs brought a significant number of faculty, scholars, and students from other countries. Additionally, 4-H and the Cooperative Extension Service established an International Youth Farm Exchange, and Kansas State established a South Asia Studies Center.

Kansas State officially became a university during McCain's tenure. In *Kansas State University: The Quest for Identity*, historian James Carey explains that McCain resisted when students first suggested the name change. He worried the college would lose its identify as a land-grant school and its accompanying annual appropriations. But when students persisted, administrators endorsed the idea, and Faculty Senate voted in favor of achieving university status, McCain agreed to the name change. The Kansas House voted unanimously to change the institution's name to Kansas State University of Agriculture and Applied Science. Governor George Docking signed the bill in February 1959.

The KSU Endowment and Alumni Association conducted business from the Hollis House located on the northeast corner of Claflin Road and Denison Avenue, early 1970s. A former fraternity house, the organizations used the building as headquarters for more than twenty years.

Governor George Docking signs the 1959 bill that changed the college's name to Kansas State University of Agriculture and Applied Science. Witnessing the signing are (left to right) James McCain, Larry French (student council chairman), and Chuck Wingert (student body president). The name change added prestige and properly reflected the complexity of expanding programs and graduate degrees.

As one of the many active social clubs on campus, the K-State Cosmopolitan Club hosted activities such as this skating party in the 1950s. The club's main mission was to promote brotherhood among all peoples of the world through educational trips, exchange programs, conference panels, and parties.

Students enjoy relaxing at Pillsbury Crossing located southeast of Manhattan. As in the 1950s, it remains a popular gathering place today. (RP)

Bob Boozer, K-State's two-time all-American basketball player, signs autographs in 1959. Boozer was a member of the 1960 Olympic team that won the gold medal. Taken by the Cincinnati Royals, he was the first overall selection in the 1959 National Basketball Association draft.

Angel Flight members receive instruction during a tour of McConnell Air Force Base in Wichita. Primarily a service organization, Angel Flight served as the official hostess group for the Air Force ROTC and promoted good relations with the service corps.

In 1960, students take time to relax and smell the roses in the Formal Gardens, a popular place for gathering, relaxing, and wedding ceremonies. Despite protests, the Formal Gardens, located where Bluemont Hall stands today, were razed in the late 1970s for campus expansion. (RP)

Construction is underway for the departments, laboratories, classrooms, and offices for the College of Home Economics in Justin Hall. The building was named in honor of Margaret M. Justin who served as dean of home economics for thirty-one years. When opened in 1960, it was the first building on campus with central air conditioning. (RP)

A rapid increase in university enrollment for fall semester in 1960 resulted in severe overcrowding in Goodnow Hall (the new men's residence hall) requiring thirty-three students to be temporarily housed in the basement, which had no restrooms or study facilities.

Workers install the new pipe organ in All Faiths Memorial Chapel, 1961. The organ was designed by world famous organ architect James Jamison and purchased from private donations for $50,000. The chapel honors K-Staters who died in World War II and the Korean War.

A student undergoes pledge training to become a member of the Pershing Rifle group in K-State's military science program. (RP)

The tradition of selecting the Favorite Man on Campus lasted from 1946 to 1972. Coeds listened to persuasive speeches and watched skits to determine the winner. One year a candidate, ready to perform a skit with fraternity brothers, found himself alone on stage. Thinking quickly, he grabbed a guitar and sang cowboy songs. The women loved it and crowned him FMOC.

Built in 1904, many considered the two-thousand-seat Auditorium inadequate including a world famous classical guitarist who found the swinging doors, rattling windows, creaking floors, and blasts of cold air so distracting that he stood up before beginning his concert and implored, "Shut the door!"

Campus police outside the Department of Security and Traffic office on the west side of Anderson Hall.

Steel pipes brace the east wall of Anderson Hall to prevent additional damage, 1961. The wall had shifted outward and was replaced.

Alpha Phi Omega members carry Touchdown VII, a live wildcat, around the basketball court, 1962. From 1922 to 1977, the caged wildcat appeared before cheering crowds at home football and basketball games. (RP)

As part of their Greek Day festivities, K-State fraternities perform volunteer work in town such as cleaning, painting, or repairing buildings. Here they help the City of Manhattan build a sidewalk in 1961. (RP)

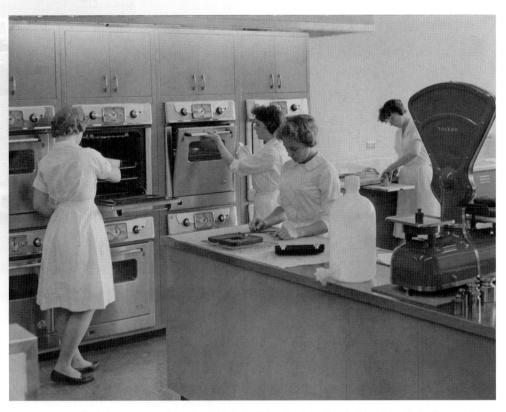

Students use commercial equipment in Justin Hall as they learn the principles of quantity food preparation in a 1962 Institutional Management class, a two-credit-hour course. Six hours of laboratory per week were required. In 1962, the College of Home Economics had 677 undergraduates and thirty-seven graduate students. (RP)

Looking west down Moro Street in Aggieville, circa 1960s. Pizza Hut (on the left) opened in 1960 and is the oldest Pizza Hut in the U.S. still operating in its original location. After purchasing the Campus Theatre in 1998 and renovating the structure, Varney's Book Store opened its new addition at 623 North Manhattan Avenue in 2000.

Part of the university's centennial celebration in 1963 included a group of senior cheerleaders and officers that affectionately called themselves the "Centennial Ceniors." Their antics included special cheers and songs as part of the pre-football game rally against KU and later at the KSU-Colorado basketball game. (RP)

A view from 17th Street and Anderson Avenue looking north shows the Student Union, Seaton Hall, Power Plant, and Memorial Stadium, 1963. The Kansas State sign (left) lists the 1963–1964 home basketball games; a banner at the bottom of the sign reads "Kansas State University CENTENNIAL, 1863, 1963."

KSU's nuclear reactor in Ward Hall (shown in 1963) operated at 100 kilowatts of thermal power when first powered up in 1962; in 2012, the reactor could operate up to 1,250 kilowatts. Kansas State is one of twenty-five universities nationwide that operate research reactors.

The KSU band marches west down Poyntz Avenue on November 17, 1963, during the Centennial Homecoming Parade. The parade route began in downtown Manhattan and finished in Aggieville. (RP)

Band majorettes pose during a 1963 KSU
football game in Memorial Stadium.

Willie the Wildcat came on the scene in 1964. The
cheerleading squad entertains the crowd during a
basketball game time-out. They used only two cheers during
the season and wore uniforms they designed. (RP)

BAND DAY 1964

KANSAS STATE UNIVERSITY   NOVEMBER 14, 1964

MANHATTAN, KANSAS

Seventy-four high school bands from across the state perform with the K-State band in 1964 during a ceremony honoring People-to-People, an international student ambassador organization envisioned by President Dwight D. Eisenhower in 1956. The "Salute to Peace" half-time program reflected People-to-People's motto: promoting peace through understanding.

President James McCain is on stage with the officer leading the ceremony as students take the oath commissioning them as officers in the U.S. Army during graduation exercises in the Auditorium, early 1960s.

President McCain and Steve Vesecky of Campbell Taggart Associated Bakeries cut a seven-foot loaf of bread at the 1964 dedication of the newly established bakery management program. KSU is the only school in the country to offer an undergraduate degree in bakery science and management, feed science and management, and milling science and management; graduate degrees and a minors program are also available.

Above: The Student Union has always hosted many programs and events. Here students rock at a dance in the ballroom after a 1964 Wildcat basketball victory over the Missouri Tigers. (RP)

Left: A member of the class of 1965, Margaret Thompson Murdock was K-State's first female Olympian and the first to win a medal in rifle shooting, taking the silver in 1976 when men and women competed against each other in the event. She is second from the left on the bottom row. (RP)

Above: As "The Barn" burned in the early morning hours of January 15, 1965, hundreds of students watched the fire and cheered when the Auditorium roof collapsed. Two music students were charged with arson. One pled guilty, the other was convicted, and both were imprisoned.

Left: Married student housing in Jardine Terrace sustains major damage during a storm on June 8, 1966. Jardine residents took shelter in closets and bathrooms, and there were no serious injuries. While many campus buildings and facilities were seriously affected, some declared total losses, Jardine Terrace suffered the most extensive damage with an estimated $3 million loss. Four hundred and fifty families had to relocate because their apartments were uninhabitable. They found temporary housing in dormitories and private apartments.

Ahearn Field House provided a venue for a variety of campus activities. Here, KSU's 1966 graduating class receives their diplomas in the field house.

Dwight D. Eisenhower, former president of the United States, receives an honorary doctor of law degree, KSU's highest honor at the time, during the 103rd commencement ceremony in 1966.

Students and faculty conduct experiments in a chemistry laboratory in Willard Hall, 1967.

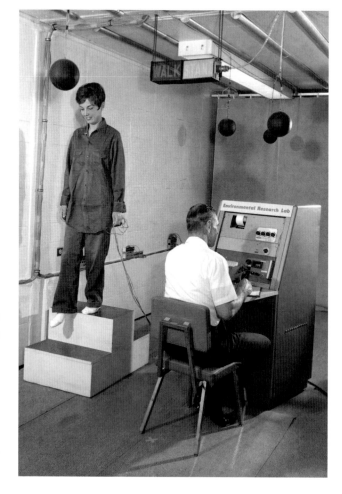

A researcher studies the thermal interaction of people and their surroundings at the Institute for Environmental Research in 1967. The interdisciplinary research program was established in 1963 with the support of the American Society of Heating, Refrigerating and Air Conditioning Engineers.

Band Director Paul Shull leads the K-State
Alumni Band in its debut performance at the
1967 homecoming game. Players rehearsed
for an hour and a half before playing an
Herb Alpert melody. Thirty-five alumni
who graduated between 1931 and 1967
participated. (*K-Stater*)

The graduating class of 1968 received
degrees in the open air of KSU's Memorial
Stadium. Looking east, one can view Calvin
Hall behind the stadium on the right and
Anderson Hall on the left.

Parking permits cost $5 in 1969 but did not guarantee a convenient parking space as shown here with students circling the K-State Union parking lot. Over the years, many proposals were considered to alleviate the campus parking problem.

Students learn speed and accuracy in a basic typing class, 1969. Juniors in the College of Commerce consulted with faculty advisors to select fields of specializations. Students specializing in secretarial studies had to take Typewriting I and II as well as Shorthand I, a four-credit-hour course. (RP)

In 1970 a new auditorium was completed. To dedicate the facility, Gail Kubik, composer in residence, was commissioned to write a musical score for the event. Kubik's "A Record of Our Time" was performed by the Minnesota Symphony Orchestra. Shown (left to right) are Rod Walker, choral director; Gail Kubik; Ray Milland, narrator; and George Trautwein, conductor. The auditorium was named after President James McCain in 1975. (Gail Kubik Papers)

Aerial view of KSU Stadium and surrounding area looking east in 1970. The stadium was completed in 1968.

More than a dozen restaurants were located in Aggieville in the early 1970s, many of which have come and gone, including Mr. K's at 710 North Manhattan Avenue and the Mar Cafe at 708 North Manhattan.

Students, like these in 1974, camp out in front of Ahearn Field House to get basketball tickets for choice seats on a first come, first served basis; camping out for tickets was a long-standing tradition when the Wildcats played in Ahearn.

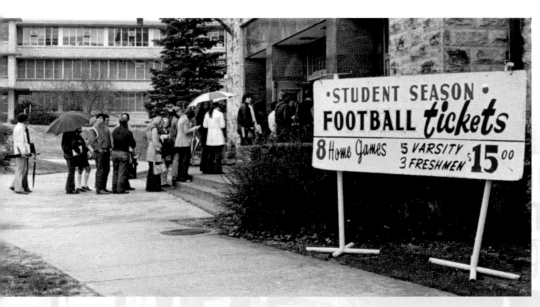

Students line up outside Ahearn Field House to purchase season football tickets, circa 1974.

Student unrest in the 1960s brought dissatisfaction with society, the educational system, political conditions, racial discrimination, and military involvement overseas. At Kansas State, well-meaning students along with radicals protested on campus; demonstrators against the Vietnam War targeted the ROTC program resulting in minor skirmishes.

In 1968 when both Martin Luther King Jr. and Robert Kennedy were assassinated within months of their speaking engagements at Kansas State, the climate of unrest worsened. On December 12, following a stormy meeting with students, African-American leaders, and administrators in the Student Union, McCain placed the campus on alert but to no avail——the next night, arsonists burned Nichols Gym. While there were racial issues on campus during this period, they were not as divisive as elsewhere in the country. African-American students, along with white students, often confronted administrators about mutual concerns. Minor incidents continued but few students and faculty supported those behind the violence and destruction that transpired.

Above: Students gather in the K-State Union to listen to a speaker protesting the war in Vietnam, 1972.

Right: A group of student activists offered an opportunity to sign a 1971 petition asking members of the Kansas congressional delegation to explain their support for military expansion into Laos as part of the American involvement in Vietnam.

Dr. Martin Luther King Jr., Nobel Peace Prize winner and civil rights leader, on stage in Ahearn Field House before his University Convocation address, "The Future of Integration." His speech on January 19, 1968, turned out to be his last to a university audience before his assassination a few months later.

Two days after announcing his run for the presidency, Senator Robert F. Kennedy gives his first campaign speech during a Landon Lecture at KSU, 1968. Ethel Kennedy (seated) accompanied her husband to a packed Ahearn Field House. Just seventy-nine days later, Kennedy was assassinated. The "Rocky" banners refer to the Republican candidate, Nelson Rockefeller.

During the period of unrest on the nation's campuses, arsonists set fire to Nichols Gym on Friday, December 13, 1968. Comments about burning the university had been made the previous evening at a contentious faculty-student meeting regarding student concerns. Nichols Gym was home to KSAC

Throughout the late 1960s and 1970s, diversity increased on campus. Grain science professor Robert J. Johnson achieved status as the most senior African-American faculty member. Alumnus Veryl Switzer, a former All-American football player, became associate dean for minority affairs, a newly created position. African-American homecoming queens reigned in 1968 and 1972, and the first African-American student body president was elected in 1975. The number of African-American, Mexican-American, and Native-American students reached all-time highs. Several activities, including Black Awareness Week, promoted racial equality and the university established a Minorities Resource and Research Center in Farrell Library. A Commission on the Status of Women and an affirmative action program addressed gender discrimination. Although inequalities in the number of female and male faculty members and their salaries remained, the gap narrowed.

Above: Gordon Parks, nationally known photographer, author, motion picture director, and composer, visits the Minority Resource Research Center in Farrell Library while on campus in 1973. With Parks is Alvin Lewis, head of the center and instructor in the Department of Family and Child Development.

Below: In 1953, All-American running back Veryl Switzer leads the Wildcats in rushing with 558 yards. The Green Bay Packers drafted Switzer in 1954. He returned to KSU in 1973 to become assistant vice president for minority affairs. In 1988 he was appointed associate athletic director for academics and now serves as associate athletics director emeritus.

President Richard Nixon arrives by helicopter north of Ahearn Field House to deliver the fourteenth Landon Lecture on September 16, 1970. Nixon is on the right shaking hands with Governor Robert Docking and Mrs. Nixon is shaking hands with Mrs. Alf Landon. KSU was considered one of the safest college campuses for the president to visit since anti-Vietnam War sentiment in the country was high. Nixon was the first sitting president to visit K-State and provided the university with considerable national exposure.

With the establishment of the Alf Landon Lecture Series on Public Issues in 1967, notable speakers visited Kansas State, none more prominent than President Richard Nixon on September 16, 1970. The crowd of over sixteen thousand cheered enthusiastically though a few hecklers could be heard criticizing Nixon for his role in escalating the war in Southeast Asia. The presidential visit brought national publicity for Kansas State, probably the most the institution ever received.

Kansas State succeeded in becoming a comprehensive university under the administrations of Milton Eisenhower and James McCain. No longer operating under the narrow definition of a land-grant institution, Kansas State transformed into a modern research university with nationally recognized programs and an expanded international presence.

— Anthony R. Crawford

For sources, see the following:

Ambrose, Stephen E. and Richard H. Immerman. *Milton S. Eisenhower: Educational Statesman*. Baltimore: Johns Hopkins University Press, 1983 (Chapters 6–7).

Carey, James C. *Kansas State University: The Quest for Identity*. Lawrence: Regents Press of Kansas, 1977 (Chapters 8–12).

Eisenhower, Milton S. *Report to Kansas: An Account of Seven Years of Stewardship*. Manhattan: Kansas State College, 1950

Kansas State Collegian (newspaper, 1943–1975).

McCain, James A. *The 1950s at Kansas State University: Report of a Decade of Progress*. Manhattan: Kansas State University, 1960.

McCain, James A. *Decade of the Sixties: Kansas State University, Ten Years of Progress*. Manhattan: Kansas State University, c.a. 1960.

Quiring, Virginia, ed. *The Milton S. Eisenhower Years at Kansas State University*. Manhattan: Friends of the Libraries of Kansas State University, 1986.

Royal Purple (college yearbook, 1943–1975).

University Archives (Subject Files: newspaper and periodical articles, reports, ephemera).

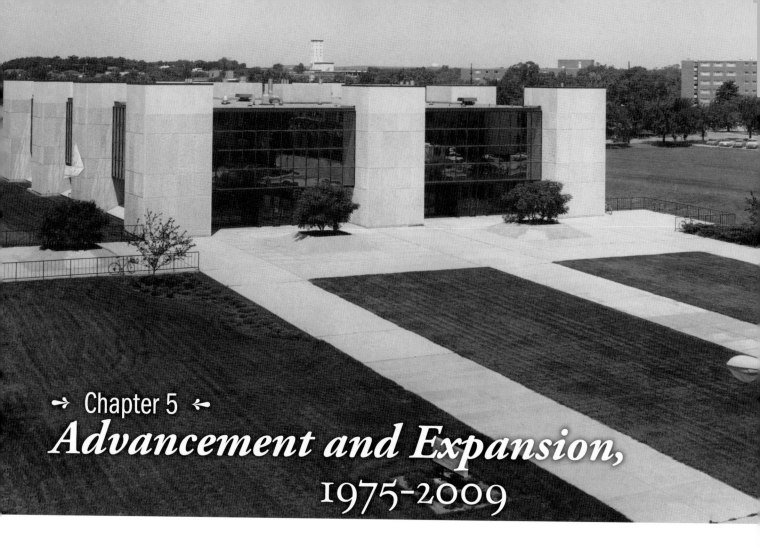

→ Chapter 5 ←
Advancement and Expansion,
1975–2009

Above: Completed in 1976, Durland Hall (Merrill A. Durland) was the first of three building phases for the College of Engineering. Additions were completed in 1983 (Donald Rathbone Hall) and 2000 (George Fiedler Hall). The structure with its windows and building materials was designed to reflect solar heat in the summer and absorb it in the winter.

Right: Duane Acker (left) visits with his predecessor, James A. McCain. Acker, KSU's eleventh president, held the office for eleven years, 1975–1986.

After much fanfare, James A. McCain retired in 1975. From an applicant pool of approximately three hundred, the Board of Regents hired Duane Acker, Kansas State's eleventh president. Acker's experience with land-grant colleges came from his advanced degrees in animal science (Iowa State University and Oklahoma State University). He also held positions in agriculture at four land-grants, including Kansas State (associate dean of agriculture and director of resident instruction, 1962–1966).

Acker with Randall Hildebrand and Debra Rolph after they were announced as the new K-State Ambassadors during the 1983 homecoming football game. (*K-Stater*)

Duane and Shirley Acker visit the Richard L. D. and Marjorie J. Morse Department of Special Collections in 2011. Acker used the records of his presidency in the University Archives to write a book about his experience, *Two at a Time: Reflections and Revelations of a Kansas State University Presidency and the Years that Followed*, published in 2010.

Continued growth in the physical plant during Acker's administration included the planning or construction of at least ten new buildings. These facilities represented expansion in engineering, human ecology, international students, veterinary medicine, athletics, education, chemistry, and agriculture.

Above: Elected the first African-American student body president in February 1975, Bernard Franklin used a grassroots write-in campaign to defeat his closest opponents in a field of four by over 1,300 votes. Amy Button (Renz), now CEO of the Kansas State Alumni Association, was third in the voting. Franklin graduated in 1976 and in 1978 he was named to the Kansas Board of Regents making him the youngest member ever appointed.

Top Left: Theresa Perenich, head of the Department of Clothing, Textiles, and Interior Design, served as the first female president of Faculty Senate from 1976 to 1977. Prior to coming to KSU, she worked as a chemistry researcher on the University of Florida's *Gatorade* project.

Left: Sam Brownback as a senior at Kansas State when he served as president of the student body, 1978–1979. After graduating in 1979 with a degree in agricultural economics, he held multiple state governing positions, including agricultural secretary. Brownback was elected to the U.S. House in 1994 and won a seat in the U.S. Senate in 1996 followed by a second term. He was elected the forty-sixth governor of Kansas in 2010.

One construction project, the rebuilding of Nichols Gym, caused controversy. Most administrators favored demolishing the burned-out shell. Acker agreed and submitted a proposal to Kansas legislators to raze Nichols. Students, faculty, alumni, and state officials immediately launched a crusade to "Save the Castle." Acker backed off but charged those supporting reconstruction to find the funding necessary to rebuild. They did and a restored Nichols Hall was dedicated in 1986.

The "Save Me" sign painted on the boarded-up entrance to Nichols Gym reflects the sentiment of many people on campus.

Opposite Page: When Duane Acker became president he inherited the burned-out shell of Nichols Gym, home to KSAC radio and the music department, which lost over $500,000 in instruments and music in the blaze, some of which are shown here.

Right: On September 29, 1975, President Acker met with students at their request in front of Nichols Gym regarding the future of the structure. "Rebuild the Castle" was one of the slogans used by those in support of saving Nichols. Behind Acker is Chris Badger from Student Senate and to his right is Kent Foerster, who invited Acker to speak, with Bernard Franklin behind him.

Below: Duane Acker speaking at the "Rebuild the Castle" rally in front of Nichols Gym. To the left is Kent Foerster, undergraduate student in political science and son of Bernd Foerster, dean of architecture. To Acker's right in the photograph is Bernard Franklin, student body president, and Chris Badger, from Student Senate.

In the late 1970s, the seating capacity of Ahearn Field House could not be expanded, so interest in a new basketball arena grew. Some thought the lack of a modern facility had also adversely affected recruiting. Debates over feasibility studies and questions about cost plagued efforts to construct a building with a 16,000-seat capacity. Ultimately, an increase in student fees and gifts from private sources, including major donor Fred Bramlage, helped fund a scaled back coliseum, which opened in 1988.

Acker left Kansas State confident in the financial integrity of athletics and that programs complied with NCAA and conference rules (previously, a probation and ban had plagued the football team). Part of Acker's legacy included the football team playing in its first bowl game (the Independence Bowl) and the advancement of Title IX and women's athletics. Kansas State combined women's and men's programs into one department, making it the first university in the Big 8 to obtain a greater equality in the number of intercollegiate sports for women and men.

Right: Judy Akers became KSU's first women's basketball coach in 1968. During her eleven years at the helm, her teams won over two hundred games and two conference titles. She led the way in implementing equality in men's and women's athletics at KSU after Title IX became law in 1972. She served as women's athletics director from 1974 to 1976 and remains the university's second winningest coach behind Deb Patterson.

Below: A celebration in the locker room after the Wildcats defeat the Colorado Buffaloes to win an invitation to play in the 1982 Independence Bowl. Reveling in the moment are (left to right) Coach James Dickey, Athletics Director Dick Towers, President Duane Acker, and Kansas governor and KSU alum John Carlin. The Cats lost to Wisconsin (14-3) in their first bowl game appearance.

Above: In 1986, jubilant KSU fans gathered in Aggieville to wildly celebrate their win over the University of Kansas after the Wildcat football team beat the Jayhawks 29-12. In addition to multiple broken shop windows, the raucous crowd destroyed an automobile. Workers cleaned up the damage to stores on Moro Street the morning after the riot. (RP).

Top Left: Fans, such as this one, expressed their frustration with KSU's losing football team in the mid 1980s. K-State won a total of four games during the 1985 through 1989 seasons (winless in 1987 and 1988).

Left: Chester Peters, vice president for student affairs (left), and Art Stone, director of the K-State Police Department, disperse a rowdy crowd that tore down the goal posts after KSU's win over the University of Kansas in 1984. Peters was dean of students/vice president for student affairs from 1954 to 1985. In 1995, KSU honored Peters's service by naming the student recreation center in his honor. (RP)

Administrative changes credited to Acker included establishing the position of provost, employing the first minority vice president, combining finances and facilities under one vice president, and placing agricultural programs under one dean. Academic advances included the establishment of master's level studies in fine arts, an interdepartmental program in recreation, an undergraduate dance major, a dairy research and teaching center, as well as the College of Engineering's centers for energy and occupational safety and health. A cooperative agreement with Nebraska offered its residents in-state tuition rates for veterinary medicine.

Owen Koeppe, shown in the Great Room of Farrell (now Hale) Library, was appointed provost by President Duane Acker in 1980. Koeppe served as the university's first provost from 1980 to 1987. (RP)

The musical *Cabaret* was part of the K-State Players performance series in McCain Auditorium in 1982. According to the *Collegian*, the performance included elaborate stage sets, orchestra pit, and bizarre costume designs to create a production that was "exciting, entertaining, and thought provoking." (K-State Players).

Students in assistant professor Teresa Schmidt's 1982 art class work on nude figure drawings. Models, according to many students, provide the kind of diversity in form, shape, and proportion necessary to grow as artists. (RP)

Thomas Richardson, radio and television major, prepares a record album to play on KSDB, KSU's radio station located in McCain Auditorium, 1985. (RP)

Like Eisenhower and McCain, Acker expanded international programs both on campus and abroad. The College of Business created the International Trade Institute, the College of Agriculture developed international programs in grains and livestock, and an International Student Center was built. Kansas State initiated agricultural projects in Nigeria, Botswana, and the Philippines.

Above: Professor of Agriculture Barry Flinchbaugh (left) and Marc Johnson (right), head of the Department of Agricultural Economics, address farmers' concerns over the 1986 Farm Bill. Kansas members of the American Agricultural Movement organized rallies on campus and elsewhere after Flinchbaugh suggested in speeches that most Kansas farmers believed the agricultural crisis was highly exaggerated.

Right: Former Kansas governor and 1936 presidential candidate Alf Landon seen here at a Landon Lecture in 1980. The Landon Lecture Series on Public Issues, named in honor of the former governor, continues as one of the most prestigious of its kind in the country.

Far Right: Students attend a 1984 Division of Continuing Education (DCE) introduction class on microcomputers. Intended for students fifty-five years of age or older, DCE often worked with other associations such as the North Central Flint Hills Area Agency and the Older Kansas Employment Program to provide workers with skills in a changing job market. (DCE)

While enrollment reached 19,982 in 1981, the number of students attending Kansas State began to drop in the following years. In an effort to reverse the trend, Acker encouraged the Kansas State Alumni Association to hire a student recruitment staff member and open an office in Kansas City. Scholarship awards increased from $293,000 in 1975 to $1.4 million in 1984. Kansas State began awarding National Merit Scholarships with nine semi-finalists in 1977 and fifty-five in 1985.

At a time when insufficient state appropriations for higher educations declined, fundraising increased from $10.6 million in 1975 to $44.5 million in 1985. Membership in the President's Club, a key philanthropic support group whose members contributed at least $10,000, grew from 140 to 840 donors.

Acker stepped down as president in 1986. During his tenure, some criticized Acker's handling of difficult issues, but his departure generated mainly positive publicity giving him credit for eleven years of progress. Perhaps Earle Davis, retired chair of the English department, said it best: "Most think Acker did a lot of good for K-State and should be recognized for his accomplishments—even if some disagreed once in a while."

KSU organizes an All-University Open House parade in 1982 to introduce potential students and their families to campus departments, faculty, groups, and activities. Originally established by a group of engineering students in 1920 as an Engineering Day Open House, KSU continues the tradition by engaging prospective students with festive events and academic displays in the spring.

Gwendolyn Brooks, winner of the Pulitzer Prize for Poetry, visits the Minorities Resource Research Center in Farrell (now Hale) Library during a trip to KSU in 1983. Brooks discussed the importance of poetry in society and encouraged students to claim their education. She returned in 1985 to present a university convocation on the legacy of Martin Luther King Jr.

Registration table for University for Man classes in the K-State Union, early 1980s. Now known as the UFM Community Learning Center, the organization was established in 1968 by students and faculty as a way for people on campus and area residents to interact through classes, programs, and services.

Nina Miley leans over the doughnut display table to serve student customers at "Swannies." The legendary downtown pastry shop was part of the student-life routine for many years. In the evenings after the store "officially" closed to the public, students and Manhattanites could still purchase late-night pastries by entering through the back alley.

A campus posting in 1981 tells students and faculty to take a moment of remembrance on the one-year anniversary of John Lennon's murder on December 8, 1980. Lennon gained fame as one of the Beatles in the 1960s before going solo and marrying artist and peace activist Yoko Ono.

Residents of KSU's Marlatt Hall participate in a popular 1980s campus craze of seeing how many people could fit into a telephone booth.

The Ecumenical Christian Ministries at 1021 Denison Avenue, circa 1980, included several campus ministries to encourage "students to explore their spiritual beliefs through fellowship, study, and service."

COMPUTING AND
INFORMATION
SCIENCES

Above: University administrators and faculty recognize a major donation from American Telephone & Telegraph Company for computer equipment in 1988. The Departments of Computing and Information Sciences and Electrical and Computer Engineering were the direct beneficiaries. Shown in Nichols Hall is Clo Whitaker of AT&T, President Jon Wefald, and Virgil Wallentine, head of computer sciences. Over several years AT&T donated $3 million worth of hardware to KSU.

Right: Physics professor Dean Zollman teaches a course for the Division of Continuing Education. Organized in 1966, DCE provides educational opportunities for students, adult learners, and working professionals. Its first online course was offered in 1996. (DCE)

Gordon Jump (1932–2003), KSU journalism and mass communications major and a member of the class of 1957, is being interviewed by a broadcast journalism student. Jump is most known for his role as radio station manager "Arthur Carlson" in the television show *WKRP Cincinnati* and as the infamous Maytag repairman in the company's commercials. (RP)

Steve Wolgast, *Collegian* photographer, develops a photo in the newspaper's dark room, 1987. After graduating in 1990, he held positions with several newspapers, including news design editor for the *New York Times*. In 2009, Wolgast returned to KSU and serves as director of student publications and adviser to the *Collegian* in the Miller School of Journalism and Mass Communications. (RP)

Trenetta Tubwell (left) and Lisa Rothel perform "Wait 'till Morning" for the Ebony Theatre. The African-American, student-led theater troupe went on to win the American College Theater Festival regional competition in 1989 and gained an invitation to the national competition at the Kennedy Center in New York City. Ebony Theatre, established in 1977, includes performances by African-American playwrights and actors and remains the only multicultural theater program in the Midwest.

In 1986, John Wefald succeeded Acker as Kansas State's twelfth president. His credentials appealed to various university constituencies—he held a doctorate in history and had served as Minnesota's commissioner of agriculture and as chancellor of the state's university system. Wefald's experience prepared him to address the Board of Regents' charge to increase enrollment, improve athletics, and enhance K-State's public image.

Above: President Jon Wefald picks up trash near Anderson Hall. As president, he acted as a role model to keep the university grounds looking beautiful and encouraged others to take care of their campus.

Right: President Jon Wefald and First Lady Ruth Ann at the president's house, 2008. President Wefald held office from 1986 to 2009. As first lady, Ruth Ann Wefald served KSU and the community in numerous capacities, most notably her leadership in the campaign for an art museum on campus. (GM-C&M)

To meet the enrollment challenge, Wefald established a comprehensive recruitment program focusing on attracting graduates from Kansas high schools as well as targeted areas out of state. Efforts such as increased scholarships and financial aid led to record enrollments (17,630 in 1986 to 23,520 in 2008). In the area of student achievement Wefald helped expand the number of national scholarships awarded, such as Rhodes, Truman, Marshall, Goldwater, and Udall, eventually placing Kansas State first among five hundred public universities.

President Jon Wefald shown with Rhodes Scholar Vincent Hofer, holding a sweatshirt with his name and the date he received the honor in 2008. KSU ranks high in the number of public universities with Rhodes Scholar recipients. (DM-C&M)

Former President Bill Clinton (right) and Landon Lecture Series Chairman Charles Reagan visit on stage before Clinton's remarks. In his 2007 lecture at Bramlage Coliseum, Clinton discussed the interconnected nature of global commerce, education, politics, and life. He was the 148th speaker in the highly acclaimed series.

As part of the Department of Grain Science and Industry's international programs, students came to KSU to attend courses in feed management, flour milling, grain marketing, and management. Associate Professor Ekraumi Haque taught this 1990 class.

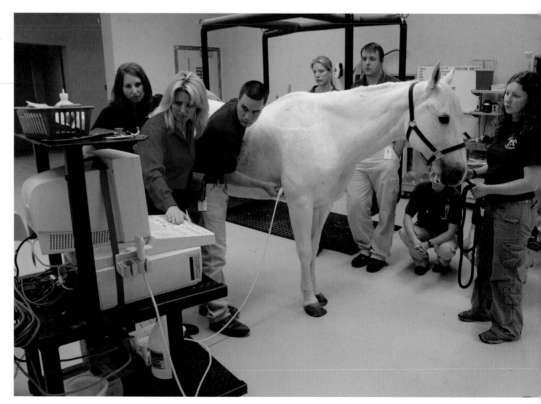

In 2006, fourth-year students in the College of Veterinary Medicine learn how to perform ultrasound examinations from Laurie Beard, associate professor in equine internal medicine. Beard is at the machine on the left. (College of Veterinary Medicine)

Left: "Take Back the Night" march in 2007 sponsored by Ordinary Women, a feminist student organization at K-State with the mission to confront injustices through activism and other means. Shown at the corner of Anderson/Bluemont Avenue and Manhattan Avenue, the annual walk traditionally began at the K-State Union and ended in City Park where presentations were made.

Below Left: Members of Chi Omega enjoy sorority living by riding mattresses down a flight of stairs. Today twenty sororities and twenty-seven fraternities make up the Greek system at K-State.

Below: Performing in KSU Stadium after Austin Peay University defeated the Wildcats on a rainy Labor Day Weekend in 1987, Willie Nelson's concert was to bring attention to the plight of agricultural communities and to raise funds for his Farm Aid organization. The estimated ten thousand people in attendance were not enough for Farm Aid to receive any revenue from the concert. The *Collegian* reported the majority of the crowd was students and that most of the alumni, disgruntled by the outcome of the game and the rain, left the stadium.

Wefald supported academic development by strengthening the Regents Distinguished Professor program (1986:2; 2008:40) with forty new endowed positions and several faculty receiving recognition as Carnegie/CASE Foundation professors of the year. Support for research also increased (1986:$19 million; 2008:$220 million) as did overall university funding.

Above: In 1861 the college bell was purchased for Bluemont Central College. It moved to Farm Machinery Hall on the KSAC campus in 1875 and relocated to the tower of Anderson Hall when it was constructed in 1882. After eighty-three years of use, the bell was replaced with an electric carillon and remained hidden in Anderson Hall until 1995 when it was installed outside of Bluemont Hall and rededicated during the K-State Open House.

Right: Late in the evening of July 11, 2008, tornadic storms ravaged the state of Kansas. One, an EF-4, touched down outside Manhattan and tracked through the city, generating over $20 million in damage to businesses, homes, and the university, including Weber Hall shown here.

On October 31, 1990, Dean of Human Ecology Barbara Stowe led a demonstration against the proposal of the KSU administration to abolish the college as part of a reorganization plan. Students and faculty from the Colleges of Human Ecology and Architecture and Design, and others against the plan, marched through the halls of Anderson Hall shouting, "Hell no, we won't go."

Students and faculty gathered on the lawn in front of Anderson Hall on November 7, 1990, to demonstrate against a proposed university reorganization which included closing the College of Architecture and Design and the College of Human Ecology. In the foreground are architecture students with their T-squares serving as grave markers to symbolize the death of the college.

Right: In 1991 the university purchased the Kansas Farm Bureau building on Anderson Avenue for the KSU Foundation and Alumni Association. In 1995 the tower was named in honor of Arthur F. Loub, foundation president from 1979 to 1994. The KSU Alumni Association moved to its new building on campus in 2002.

Below: Engineering students completed the K on K-Hill overlooking Manhattan in 1921, followed by the S in 1930. At a later date feasibility studies determined it would be too costly to stabilize the land to the west for the letter U. Members of Tau Beta Pi, an engineering honor society, paint and maintain the letters. Shown here in 1989, "K-Hill" remains a prominent landmark.

Above: A 1987 aerial view of Bramlage Coliseum under construction (KSU Stadium to the right and Jardine Apartments, lower right). In the first basketball game at the facility in 1988, K-State defeated Purdue University. Purdue was coached by Gene Keady, a KSU 1958 graduate.

Left: After construction work ended in 1988, the newly opened Bramlage Coliseum hosted its first concert on October 1 when approximately seven thousand fans watched the Beach Boys perform.

Bill Snyder during his hiring before the 1989 football season. Even his strongest supporters could never have imagined he would orchestrate the greatest turn around in college football history by taking a team that had gone winless in twenty-seven straight games to two conference championships and thirteen bowl appearances by the end of the 2012 season. With Coach Snyder at the podium in 1989 are (left to right) President Jon Wefald and Steve Miller, athletics director, who convinced others to name Snyder as K-State's thirty-second football coach.

In athletics, the football team had recorded only two winning seasons since 1954 and lost every game in 1987 and 1988. Wefald listened to athletic director Steve Miller and hired Bill Snyder. As Wildcat fans know, Snyder took a losing team and turned it into a perennial powerhouse. This transformation played a role in Kansas State becoming a member of the Big 12 Conference in 1996. The university's image improved with the football team's successes along with better records in basketball and other sports. However, Wefald received criticism in 2008 due to a contract controversy with football coach Ron Prince and questionable circumstances surrounding the position of athletic director. The rehiring of legendary coach Bill Snyder repaired some of the damage, but the situation tarnished the president's legacy.

Willie the Wildcat helps students throw a Jayhawk banner into a homecoming bonfire at a 1989 pep really held in Memorial Stadium. Unfortunately the enthusiasm did not last as K-State lost to the University of Kansas, 21-16. (RP)

At the last basketball game played in Ahearn Field House on March 5, 1988, university officials and fans joined in saying farewell to the "old barn" and honoring K-State's legendary coaches. Left to right are: President Jon Wefald; Barbara Kruger (wife of basketball coach Lon Kruger [1986–1990], who was with the team in the locker room); Jack Hartman (1970–1986); Lowell "Cotton" Fitzsimmons (1968–1970); Tex Winter (1954–1968); Jack Gardner (1939–1942, 1946–1953); and Athletics Director Larry Travis. The Cats defeated Missouri, 92-82, and moved to Bramlage Coliseum in 1988.

ESPN football analyst Lee Corso adorns a Willie the
Wildcat mascot head on national television during
"Game Day" coverage in Manhattan prior to the
1998 K-State/Nebraska football game. Corso's
prediction was correct: Wildcats 40, Nebraska 30.

The first football game played in the new Big 12 Conference took place at KSU Stadium against Texas Tech on August 31, 1996; the Wildcats won 21-14. (K-State Athletics)

Players and fans celebrate KSU's 29-28 victory over Nebraska on a cold, wintery Saturday night at KSU Stadium in November of 2000. The Huskers were ranked number four in the country, the highest ranked team ever defeated by the Cats.

Wildcats raise the Big 12 Championship trophy after defeating the number one ranked University of Oklahoma Sooners at Arrowhead Stadium in Kansas City on December 3, 2003. (K-State Athletics)

Members of the 2003 volleyball team celebrate winning the Big 12 Conference title. Led by All-Americans Lauren Goehring and Gabby Green, the Wildcats finished the season 30-5, ranked eleventh nationally, and won the program's first-ever conference championship with an 18-2 league mark. (K-State Athletics)

Members of the women's basketball team raise the 2008 Big 12 Championship trophy after winning its second conference title and first outright league crown. Head Coach Deb Patterson was selected Big 12 Coach of the Year and Kimberly Dietz and Shalee Lehning were named to the All-Big 12 first team, while Marlies Gipson received second team honors. (K-State Athletics)

Colbert Hills, located in northwest Manhattan, opened in 2000. Jim Colbert, KSU graduate (political science, 1964) and professional golfer, designed the PGA-rated course to serve the golf team, public, and university, including K-State's turf management bachelor's degree program.

Left: A beam uncovered in the basement of Holton Hall while it was being renovated in 1988 revealed the scores of several athletic events. As recorded on the beam, in 1906 the football team defeated the Jayhawks 6-4 and the next year the Wildcats defeated the KU baseball team in a double header, 4-3 and 6-5.

Below: Holton Hall, previously known as the Agriculture Building and then Education Hall, was renovated and rededicated in 1989 to house many of the services provided through the Office of Student Life. Warnings were sprayed on the walls, presumably by the contractors, in an effort to keep people from entering the construction zone. The building is named for Edwin L. Holton who served as head of the Department of Education.

The expansion of the KSU library was a topic on campus in the late 1980s and early 1990s. Although the Wefald administration supported new construction, a coalition of students, administrators, and private donors was required to devise a funding strategy acceptable to state officials. A student group, SHELF (Students Helping Enhance Library Funding) held a sit-in in Farrell Library to publicize the need for improvements and financial support. At a press conference SHELF leaders (left to right) Janelle Larson, Todd Johnson, and Ray Kowalczewski, along with Dean of Libraries Brice Hobrock, respond to questions about the future of a library addition.

Dedication ceremonies in October 1997 upon the completion of Hale Library. Standing outside of the library are (left to right): Virginia Quiring, assistant dean of libraries; Brice Hobrock, dean of libraries; Jackie McClaskey, student body president when students approved library funding; Todd Johnson, 1989–1990 student body president; Tim Riemann, current student body president; Ruth Ann Wefald; James Coffman, provost; Richard L. D. Morse, chair of the library's fundraising campaign; and Jon Wefald, president.

Hale Library functions as a gathering spot as well as a study place for students. Here students and faculty watch the first inauguration of President Barack Obama on a big screen television provided for the occasion on the second floor. (K-State Libraries Communications and Marketing)

During Wefald's tenure, Kansas State constructed twenty-six new buildings on campus and added agricultural centers in Hays and Parsons. New high profile structures on campus included the Peters Recreation Center addition, Hale Library, Alumni Center, and renovation of the Jardine apartment complex. Ruth Ann Wefald also contributed to campus expansion with her efforts to make the Marianna Kistler Beach Museum of Art a reality. In 1991, Kansas State added a campus in Salina, formerly known as the Kansas College of Technology. And by the time he left office in 2009, Wefald's administration completed plans for a new campus in Olathe and spearheaded the selection of Kansas State as the site for the National Bio and Agro-Defense Facility (NBAF). These developments highlight Kansas State's commitment to vital scientific research and development.

— Anthony R. Crawford

For sources, see the following:

Acker, Duane. *Two at a Time: Reflections and Revelations of a Kansas State University Presidency and the Years that Followed.* New York: iUniverse, 2010.

Kansas State Collegian (newspaper, 1975–2009).

Royal Purple (college yearbook, 1975–2009).

Shoop, Robert J. *A University Renaissance: Jon Wefald's Presidency at Kansas State.* Manhattan: Ag Press, 2001.

University Archives (Subject Files: newspaper and periodical articles, reports, ephemera).

Kansas State University

→ Chapter 6 ←

Initiating a New Generation, 2009-2013

Kansas State inaugurates Kirk Schulz as the university's thirteenth president on September 24, 2009. Regent Jarold Boettcher (Class of 1963) congratulates Schulz during the ceremony. (DM-C&M)

In June 2009, Kirk Schulz succeeded Jon Wefald as Kansas State University's thirteenth president. With a doctorate in chemical engineering from Virginia Tech and his tenure as Mississippi State University's vice president for research and economic development, Schulz brought an informed vision to move the university forward.

Along with a strong commitment to transparency and open communication, including his frequent use of social media, Schulz arrived with a visionary goal: "By 2025, Kansas State University will be recognized as one of the nation's Top 50 Public Research Universities." To accomplish this ambition, Schulz and the university launched an extensive strategic planning process built around seven themes: (1) research, scholarly, and creative activities and discovery, (2) undergraduate educational experience, (3) graduate scholarly experience, (4) engagement, extension, outreach, and service, (5) faculty and staff, (6) facilities and infrastructure, and (7) athletics.

To build his administration, Schulz hired April Mason as provost and senior vice president, the first woman to hold the office. He appointed new cabinet members including an athletics director and hired deans as positions opened. Part of the effort included establishing the Division of Communications and Marketing to strengthen the university's visibility. New branding strategies offered a uniform message to enhance public relations across all campuses. In December 2012, the Council for the Advancement and Support of Education (CASE) recognized President Schulz with the Chief Executive Leadership Award for his accomplishments and contributions to higher education at the national level.

President Kirk and First Lady Noel Schulz show their purple pride in Justin Hall's new addition with their sons Andrew (left) and Tim, 2012. (DM-C&M)

Left: Noel Schulz, Paslay Professor of Electrical and Computer Engineering, with her Senior Seminar in Leadership Studies. Her research interests are in power systems operations, shipboard power systems, and intelligent system applications. Schulz holds a doctorate in electrical engineering from the University of Minnesota. (DM-C&M)

Far Left: Provost April Mason joined President Schulz's administrative team in January 2010. One of her major responsibilities is directing K-State's 2025 plan to become one of the nation's top fifty public research universities. Here she speaks at a commencement ceremony for the College of Business Administration. (DM-C&M)

These initiatives and others have brought the university continued success. The *Princeton Review* listed Kansas State as one of the nation's "best colleges," giving the university high marks in the categories for campus and community relations, best quality of life, happiest students, and best run colleges. It also rated Kansas State as one of the "Best Value Colleges." Professional organizations have recognized numerous colleges, departmental programs, and faculty for their achievements. For example, Kansas State has more national CASE/Carnegie Professors of the Year than any other public research university in America. Enrollment continued to set records with a total 23,180 at the Manhattan, Salina, and Olathe campuses in Spring 2013. The number of international, African-American, and Hispanic students also increased substantially.

Above: Students in the Department of Aviation at Kansas State Salina earn degrees and certificates in aviation maintenance, avionics, professional pilot, and unmanned aircraft systems. In 1991, the Kansas College of Technology merged with Kansas State becoming the university's College of Technology and Aviation. (DM-C&M)

Background: Kansas State's newest campus, K-State Olathe, opened in 2011 and is home to the International Animal Health and Food Safety Institute. The graduate level courses offered there prepare students for careers in the biosciences and biotechnology. Located in the Kansas Bioscience Park, K-State Olathe is the first higher education facility supported by a local tax, one paid by Johnson County residents. (DM-C&M)

An ROTC cadet standing at Kansas State's Vietnam Memorial. The Department of Aerospace Studies conducts a twenty-four-hour silent watch every Veterans Day as a tribute to K-Staters who died in action during the Vietnam War. Students contributed $22,000 towards construction of the memorial, which is located near the Marianna Kistler Beach Museum of Art. (DM-C&M)

K-State's commitment to internationalism continued with the establishment of an office in Vietnam. The university reached new exchange program agreements at the University of Queensland and the University of Western Australia. In November 2010, Schulz led a delegation of K-Staters to Iraq as guests of Major General Vincent Brooks (First Infantry Division, Fort Riley).

President Kirk Schulz and Major General Vincent Brooks sign the K-State–Ft. Riley Partnership Resolution in 2009 pledging the university and the military base will engage in cooperative programs—the only such arrangement in the United States. Applauding (left to right) are Yar Ebadi, Charles Reagan, Carol Brooks, and Sergeant Major James Champagne. In 2013, KSU received a top ranking as a "military friendly" institution for soldiers and their families from the Military Advanced Education organization for the fifth consecutive year. (DM-C&M)

Preservice teacher Mattithayah Tillotson instructs USD 383 Manhattan-Ogden students in a roller coaster physics course during the summer 2012 STEM Institute. The College of Education and school district partnered to provide nearly two hundred students with fun and educational experiences in science, technology, engineering, and math (STEM fields). (Mary Hammel)

Students gather for class in the School of Leadership Studies' Campus Creek Amphitheater. Leadership studies is a popular interdisciplinary minor for students interested in civic engagement and service-learning activities. The leadership studies building opened in 2010 and received Leadership in Energy & Environmental Design (LEED) certification. (DM-C&M)

Fort Riley's U.S. Army Honor Guard participates in the dedication of Kansas State's World War II Memorial Plaza on May 30, 2011. The monument features the "Tags of Honor" sculpture surrounded by bronze plaques—"By Land; By Sea; By Air." It is located on the north side of McCain Auditorium. Governor Sam Brownback is at the podium. (DM-C&M)

Support for K-State comes from various sources. The Kansas State Alumni Association ranks number one in the Big 12 as having more graduates than any other school in the conference as members. Record financial contributions benefitted numerous programs including newly endowed faculty positions. Students, through their K-State Proud campaign, also raised considerable funds to provide financial assistance for their classmates.

Amy Button Renz, president and CEO of the K-State Alumni Association, expresses her appreciation to the K-State Marching Band for their hard work in Memorial Stadium during their summer camp in 2009. They adjourned to the Alumni Center's patio for refreshments, a tradition that began in 2002 when Renz noticed the band practicing in the August heat. (Alumni Association)

Left: Students representing various colleges participate in the 2013 Telefund at the KSU Foundation building. Dean of Human Ecology Virginia Moxley visits with Rutherford Sanford IV, a hotel and restaurant management major. Early in FY13 student representatives had already received $1.9 million in pledges for their respective colleges. (MB-C&M)

Below: K-State Proud members celebrate their seventh successful fundraising campaign. By 2013, the group had distributed $650,000 through Student Opportunity Awards to help financially disadvantaged students who have exhausted all other means for support. (MB-C&M)

A renovated and expanded Justin Hall opens in 2012 to accommodate the College of Human Ecology's growing programs. Justin Hall was built in 1960 when the college had six hundred students. Today, 2,500 students enjoy the new classrooms and study lounges. Alumni and friends of the college financed the building addition. (DM-C&M)

The physical growth of the campus also kept an impressive pace. The university successfully completed projects started before 2009 and planned new ones. Examples include ongoing work on the Jardine complex, the National Bio and Agro-Defense Facility (NBAF) site, and expansion of the Department of Grain Science and Industry facilities, the Peters Recreation Complex, and Justin Hall. Athletics has a new basketball training facility and the West Stadium Center. In 2011, an innovative campus opened in Olathe's Kansas Bioscience Park. Future construction plans include a modern and relocated Purple Masque Theater, a welcome center in Memorial Stadium-East, a new building for the College of Business, and an addition to the College of Engineering complex.

Construction is underway at the National Bio and Agro-Defense Facility (NBAF) site, shown here in August 2011. Kansas State's selection as the location for the state-of-the-art research center came after a lengthy and highly competitive process. NBAF will replace the Plum Island Animal Disease Center. Kansas State's Biosecurity Research Institute (BRI) is on the lower right. (DM-C&M)

International scientists participate in the African Swine Fever Symposium held at the Biosecurity Research Institute (BRI) in May 2012. (DM-C&M)

Below: The Jardine Apartment complex offers 1,500 students a choice of housing arrangements including studios, lofts, townhomes, and newly constructed two or four bedroom lakeside apartments (shown here). In 2005, a major redevelopment project began to renovate the original units, which were built as married student housing in the late 1950s. The facility is named after K-State's seventh president, William M. Jardine. (DM-C&M)

Right: Hale Library remains one of the most beautiful architectural structures at KSU and a popular location for students to study and socialize. It was renamed Hale Library after a major addition to Farrell Library was completed in 1997. Joe and Joyce Hale, along with funding from students, were major financial contributors to the construction project. The original library, completed in 1927, retains the name Historic Farrell in honor of Francis David Farrell, the institution's eighth president, 1925–1943.

Below: After years of parking problems on campus, and several studies on how to deal with the situation, a new parking garage (completed in 2010) on the corner of 17th and Anderson provides the campus community and visitors convenient parking adjacent to the K-State Union. (DM-C&M)

Students test their skills on the recently installed forty-foot rock-climbing wall in the Chester E. Peters Recreation Complex. Student-sponsored bonds funded the rec center addition (completed in 2013), which also features an elevated running track, new weight room and cardio deck, indoor cycling, and group fitness studios. Named after the former vice president for student affairs, the original wing was completed in 1980. (MB-C&M)

C. Clyde Jones (left), first dean of the College of Business Administration, and Ali Malekzadeh, Edgerley Family Dean of the college, during the 2012 C. Clyde Run. The charity event is in honor of Jones with proceeds going to Shepherd's Crossing, a community organization that evolved out of the Manhattan Ministerial Association to provide financial assistance to area residents. (Olivia Blanco, College of Business Administration)

Joe Goode (third from left) conducts a workshop, "Writing from the Body," for students at the Marianna Kistler Beach Museum of Art (Linda Duke, museum director, is to Goode's right). In 2013, the Joe Goode Performance Group, a contemporary dance theater troupe, performed at McCain Auditorium and spent several days in residency. (Jessica Swanson, Joe Goode Performance Group)

Konza Prairie Fire Chief Gene Towne controls the preserve's annual planned burn to maintain the tallgrass prairie ecosystem. The Konza Prairie Biological Station, located in the Flint Hills south of Manhattan, was founded in 1971. KSU and the Nature Conservancy own the research area. (Jill Haukos, Konza Prairie Biological Station)

Above: Pat Bosco interacts with incoming students in the K-State Union during the summer of 2012. Since graduating from K-State in 1971, when he was student body president his senior year, Bosco has held leadership positions involving students at the university. He now serves as vice president for student life and dean of students. (DM-C&M)

Left: Former men's basketball coach Tex Winter (right) and actor Eric Stonestreet (Class of 1996) meet at Snyder Family Stadium during the football game with the University of Kansas in 2012. Former basketball coaches and players attending a reunion were introduced at halftime. The Wildcats won eight conference championships and appeared in the Final Four twice during the years Winter coached (1953–1968). Stonestreet has won two Emmy Awards for his role on ABC's *Modern Family*. (Larry Weigel)

The K-State Book Network (KSBN) selected *The Immortal Life of Henrietta Lacks* by Rebecca Skloot for the 2012 university-wide reading program. David "Sonny" Lacks (Lacks's son) and Veronica Spencer (Lacks's great-granddaughter) spoke to students and faculty about her life. Tara Coleman, KSBN co-chair and associate professor with the K-State Libraries, is on the right. (Laura Foot)

Kansas State hosted the Big 12 Conference on Black Student Government in 2013. Planning committee members, shown here enjoying the Black and White Dinner, are proud that K-State's Black Student Union has won the award for the Outstanding Big 12 Council of the Year six times in the last eight years. (Kedric Elmore)

Graduates of the College of Arts and Sciences participate in the 2012 commencement at Bramlage Coliseum to start another generation of success. (DM-C&M)

Director of Athletics John Currie, shown here with Mary Lawrence and their children (left to right) Virginia, Mary-Dell, and Jack in the Great Room of Hale Library, runs the NCAA's most financially solvent program. Currie's sound leadership gained the Wildcat Nation's trust. His accomplishments include successfully navigating conference realignment and initiating a comprehensive plan to improve athletic facilities. (DM-C&M)

The twenty-year-old Dev Nelson Press Box impoldes on December 15, 2012 during construction for the new $75 million West Stadium Center. (K-State Athletics)

Left: President Kirk Schulz makes new basketball coach Bruce Weber an official Wildcat by presenting him with a purple blazer on March 3, 2012. John Currie, director of athletics, looks on. The men's team's first season under Coach Weber was a success—they were conference co-champions and Weber was named Big 12 Coach of the Year. (K-State Athletics)

Below: Erik Kynard wins the high jump at the 2012 NCAA Outdoor Track and Field Championship. Kynard's success continued—he won the silver medal at the 2012 Summer Olympic Games in London. (Scott Weaver, K-State Athletics)

Willie the Wildcat pumps up the crowd on an evening many K-Staters will never forget; the night the Kansas State Wildcats defeated the Texas Longhorns (42-24) in Snyder Family Stadium to win the Big 12 Championship—December 1, 2012. (K-State Athletics)

The new K-State Basketball Training Facility houses two full-length practice courts, coaching offices overlooking the courts, locker rooms, a state-of-the-art weight room, and many other features that benefit both the men's and women's teams. The building opened in 2012 and cost approximately $18 million. (DM-C&M)

1863   **2013**

150

KANSAS STATE
U N I V E R S I T Y

In 2013, as K-State celebrates its sesquicentennial with many exciting activities, the last four years make it clear that the university has embarked on the next generation of success. Go Cats!

— Anthony R. Crawford

For sources, see the following:

Kansas State Collegian (newspaper, 2009–2013).

Kansas State University. Division of Communications and Marketing (press releases, 2009–2013).

Kansas State University. Office of the President: (home page: http://www.k-state.edu/president/).

Royal Purple (college yearbook, 2009–2012).

Schulz, Kirk. "State of the University." (presidential reports, 2009–2012).

University Archives: (Subject Files: newspaper and periodical articles, reports, ephemera).

The remainder of Chapter Six, "Initiating a New Generation, 2009-2013," is divided into two sections. The first contains images of K-State's sesquicentennial celebration including kickoff activities in Ahearn Field House on February 14, 2013, followed by Gala 150 at Manhattan's Hilton Garden Inn on February 15. The chapter ends with a series of "then and now" images that reflect on how Kansas State has changed from one generation to the next over the last 150 years.

Sesquicentennial Celebration

President Kirk Schulz addresses the crowd in Ahearn Field House during the sesquicentennial kickoff on February 14, 2013. (MB-C&M)

The crowd views historical displays created by departments, colleges, and programs for the sesquicentennial kickoff event in Ahearn Field House. (Gloria Freeland)

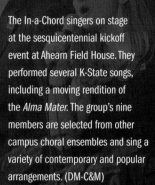

The In-a-Chord singers on stage at the sesquicentennial kickoff event at Ahearn Field House. They performed several K-State songs, including a moving rendition of the *Alma Mater*. The group's nine members are selected from other campus choral ensembles and sing a variety of contemporary and popular arrangements. (DM-C&M)

Sesquicentennial Celebration

Nathan Spriggs speaks at the opening of the sesquicentennial kickoff event in Ahearn Field House. Spriggs, an agricultural economics major, addressed the crowd in his role as the 2012–2013 student body president. (DM-C&M)

Wyatt Thompson, the "Voice of the Wildcats," and former student body presidents celebrate Kansas State's 150th birthday by singing the K-State fight song. (Left to right) Thompson, Pat Bosco (Class of 1971), Governor Sam Brownback (Class of 1979), and Jackie McClaskey (Class of 1993). (MB-C&M)

Thirty fiberglass Wildcat statues decorated by Kansas artists were displayed on campus and around Manhattan during the sesquicentennial year. At the end of the celebration, the statues were auctioned off to raise money for scholarships. They were on view at the Alumni Center February 15-17, 2013. (David D. Vail)

Above: Students serve "Wildcat Birthday 150" ice cream, a flavor created by the dairy in Call Hall exclusively for the sesquicentennial. The ice cream, filled with pieces of birthday cake and topped with royal purple sprinkles, was available only during the university's eight-month celebration. (Gloria Freeland)

Left: Jackie Hartman (left), sesquicentennial steering committee chairwoman, and Megan Umscheid, sesquicentennial project coordinator, review plans for Gala 150 and other sesquicentennial activities. (Jacinda Dent)

Sesquicentennial Celebration

Ernie Barrett ("Mr. K-State"), Laurel Littrell (professor, K-State Libraries), and Willie the Wildcat enjoy the "Wabash Cannonball" at the university's 150th birthday party in Ahearn Field House on February 14. Littrell earned her bachelor's and master's degrees in music theory and composition from KSU. She composed the sesquicentennial's orchestral fanfare, "Nature's Law," which premiered at the kickoff event. (DM-C&M)

Sesquicentennial Celebration

Above: President Kirk Schulz and Jessica Elmore, assistant director of multicultural programs for the Kansas State Alumni Association, visit at the sesquicentennial gala on February 15. (MB-C&M)

Right: The Hilton Garden Inn banquet room provides a celebratory ambiance for guests attending Gala 150. (MB-C&M)

The Kansas State seal reflects on the dance floor during Gala 150 at Manhattan's Hilton Garden Inn. (MB-C&M)

Then and Now . . .

Opposite Page Top: Nichols Gym, ca. 1915

Opposite Page Bottom: Nichols Gym with sheep on lawn, 1916

Left: Nichols Gym fire, 1968

Below: Nichols Hall, 2012 (DM-C&M)

Then and Now . . .

Aerial view of campus, 1931

Aerial view of campus, 2011 (DM-C&M)

Left: Aggieville during homecoming parade, 1938

Below: Aggieville during St. Patrick's Day parade, 2009 (Dan Walter)

Then and Now . . .

Memorial Stadium, 1933

Memorial Stadium, 2012 (MB-C&M)

Van Zile Hall, 1926

Van Zile Hall, 2012 (DM-C&M)

Then and Now . . .

Kansas State Union, 1959

Kansas State Union, 2013 (DM-C&M)

Historic Farrell Library Great Room, 1927

Historic Farrell Library Great Room, 2012

(MB-C&M)

Then and Now . . .

Historic Farrell Library Great Room mural, 1934

Artist David Overmyer standing in front of the
mural representing agriculture.

Historic Farrell Library Great Room mural, 2011

Conservator Mary Schafer working on the mural representing agriculture during a conservation project on all of the murals that was funded by Friends of the K-State Libraries.

Then and Now . . .

Konza Prairie barn as part of the Dewey Ranch, 1942

The same barn, now called Konza Prairie Biological Station Meeting Hall, 2012 (MB-C&M)

Then and Now . . .

Holton Hall, 1913

Holton Hall, 2012 (DM-C&M)

Anderson Hall, ca. 1905

Anderson Hall, 2012 (DM-C&M)

(Lauren Goc

(DM-C&M)

(DM

All-University Open House,
April 20, 2013

(MB-C&M)

Kansas State University: A Selected Chronology

1855	Isaac Goodnow and his Boston colony arrived.
1855	Trustees invited George S. Park to address them in reference to establishing an agricultural school.
1855	Cincinnati and Kansas Land Company settlers on steamer *Hartford* forced to stop in area; joined other groups in accepting Manhattan as name of the community.
1860	Bluemont Central College opened.
1861	State of Kansas admitted to the Union.
1862	Morrill Act signed by President Lincoln.
1863	Provisions of Morrill Act accepted by State of Kansas.
1863	Bluemont Central College building and one hundred acres of land deeded to the state.
1863	Joseph Denison appointed as first president of the newly organized Kansas State Agricultural College with an enrollment of twenty-six men and twenty-six women.
1867	First class graduated: five students—two men and three women.
1868	First farmers' institute held.
1873	First building erected on current campus (last known as Farm Machinery Hall).
1873	John A. Anderson appointed as Kansas State's second president.
1874	First Kansas State Alumni Association meeting held.
1875	First issue of a campus newspaper published (*Industrialist*).
1875	Shops building added to campus (oldest remaining building, now part of Seaton Complex).
1875	College instruction moved to current campus at Farm Machinery Hall and Shops Building.
1876	Holtz Hall built.
1879	George T. Fairchild appointed as Kansas State's third president.
1884	Final wing of Anderson Hall completed (north wing finished in 1879, center in 1882).
1887	Congress passed the Hatch Act, providing funding to agricultural experiment stations.
1888	Agricultural Experiment Station opened on campus.
1890	Second Morrill Act became law, with funding for instructional purposes.
1891	First yearbook published (*College Symposium*). They were intermittent until 1904 and under various titles until the 1909 *Royal Purple*.
1894	Fairchild Hall completed.
1894	Kansas State got electric lights and steam-generated heat for its buildings.
1897	Thomas E. Will appointed as Kansas State's fourth president.
1898	Kedzie Hall completed to house home economic students.
1899	First African American graduated, George Washington Owens.
1899	Ernest R. Nichols appointed as Kansas State's fifth president.
1900	Construction completed on Holton Hall.
1901	First branch agricultural experiment station established in Fort Hays, Kansas.

1901	First African-American woman graduated, Minnie M. Howell.
1904	During curricula revision, architecture was added.
1905	Four-year curriculum in veterinary medicine offered.
1906	Adams Act passed to fund research in agriculture.
1906	Garden City branch experiment station opened.
1908	Civil engineering curricula added.
1908	Council of Deans created for administration of college.
1909	Henry J. Waters appointed as Kansas State's sixth president.
1910	All curricula revised; class periods changed from fifty to sixty minutes.
1910	Engineering experiment station established.
1912	Physics department began broadcasting weather information on station 9YV.
1913	Admissions requirements raised and all curricula revised.
1913	Colby branch experiment station opened.
1914	Congress approved the Smith-Lever Act, establishing the cooperative extension service.
1917	Kansas State moved to a semester plan.
1917	Engineer's Day held, starting K-State's Open House tradition.
1918	Reserve Officers' Training Corps (ROTC) unit established.
1918	William M. Jardine appointed as Kansas State's seventh president.
1919	Kansas State created Graduate Council.
1921	The "K" was placed on Prospect Hill.
1921	Royal purple became Kansas State's official color.
1923	President's house built on Wilson Court.
1924	East wing of Memorial Stadium completed (west side completed in 1923).
1924	Campus broadcasting station KSAC, the first public radio station in Kansas, was formally created.
1925	Francis David Farrell appointed as Kansas State's eighth president.
1926	Van Zile Hall completed; the women's dorm was the first housing on campus.
1927	Farrell Library built.
1928	Kansas State accredited by the Association of American Universities.
1929	History professor Fred A. Shannon received Pulitzer Prize for *The Organization and Administration of the Union Army, 1861–1865*.
1930	The "S" was added to the "K" on Prospect Hill.
1931	Kansas State Agricultural College became Kansas State College of Agriculture and Applied Science.
1933	Kansas State conferred first PhD to Hugh Stanley Carroll in chemistry.
1935	Kansas law passed requiring male students to take two years of military training.
1939	Willard Hall opened for instruction.
1941	College Advisory Council, forerunner of the Faculty Senate, established.
1943	Milton S. Eisenhower (first alumnus and native Kansan) appointed as Kansas State's ninth president.
1943	First regular military trainees from the U.S. Air Corps arrived and an Army Specialized Training Program was established.
1944	K-State Endowment Association established.

THE

1950's

AT

KANSAS STATE UNIVERSITY

1944	No smoking rule on campus abolished.
1945	Institute of Citizenship created to aid United Nations Educational, Scientific, and Cultural Organization (UNESCO) programs.
1948	Kansas State operated first television station in the state.
1950	James A. McCain appointed as Kansas State's tenth president.
1951	Ahearn Field House construction completed.
1951	Faculty tenure system adopted.
1956	AID-India-K-State program began.
1959	Kansas State College of Agriculture and Applied Science became Kansas State University of Agriculture and Applied Science.
1960	Commencement was televised for the first time.
1961	With support from the K-State Endowment Association, a new housing area for sororities and fraternities was organized northeast of campus.
1963	Kansas State celebrated its centennial.
1965	ROTC became optional for students.
1966	Former Kansas governor and presidential candidate Alfred M. Landon delivered Kansas State's first Landon Lecture.
1968	New football stadium opened.
1968	Rev. Martin Luther King Jr. and Senator Robert Kennedy spoke on campus.
1971	Konza Prairie Research Natural Area was established.
1975	Duane C. Acker appointed as Kansas State's eleventh president.
1977	International Student Center founded.
1977	K-State Ambassadors program started.
1980	Owen J. Koeppe appointed as Kansas State's first provost.
1980	International Trade Institute founded.
1986	Jon Wefald appointed as Kansas State's twelfth president.

A MILLION STRONG . . .
. . . AND GOING STRONG

Commemorating the Acquisition of
ONE MILLION VOLUMES
by the Kansas State University Libraries
Manhattan, Kansas • April 3, 1986

1988	Bramlage Coliseum completed.
1991	Kansas College of Technology-Salina became Kansas State University-Salina Campus.
1995	K-State Football Indoor Practice Field completed.
1996	Kansas State named a Truman Scholarship Honor Institution.
1996	The Division of Continuing Education offered on-line registration and Internet courses.
1996	Nancy Landon Kassebaum received Kansas State's first Medal of Excellence.
1996	Marianna Kistler Beach Museum of Art opened.
1998	Cultural Harmony Week established.
1999	Bob Dole delivered first Huck Boyd Lecture in Community Media.
2000	Colbert Hills Golf Course opened.
2005	College of Veterinary Medicine celebrated its centennial.
2007	K-State Proud Campaign started (a student program to initiate philanthropic projects).
2008	An EF-4 tornado hit Manhattan, causing $22 million in damage to campus.
2008	Kansas State selected as the site for the National Bio and Agro-Defense Facility (NBAF).

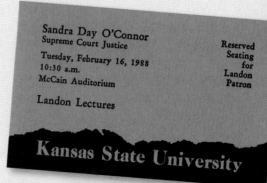

2009	Kirk Schulz appointed as thirteenth president.
2010	Department of Grain Science and Industry celebrated its centennial anniversary.
2010	A. Q. Miller School of Journalism and Mass Communications celebrated its centennial anniversary.
2011	Kansas State University Olathe opened.
2013	Kansas State celebrated its sesquicentennial anniversary.

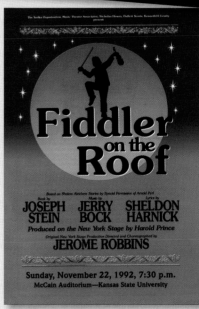

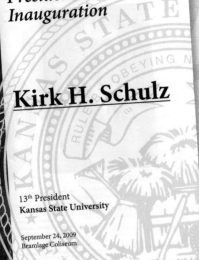

Presidential Inauguration

Kirk H. Schulz

13th President
Kansas State University

September 24, 2009
Bramlage Coliseum

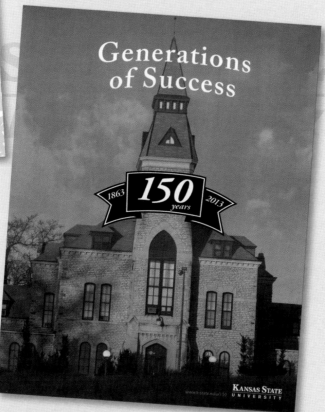

Selected Bibliography

Acker, Duane. *Two at a Time: Reflections and Revelations of a Kansas State University Presidency and the Years that Followed.* New York: iUniverse, 2010.

Ambrose, Stephen E., and Richard H. Immerman. *Milton S. Eisenhower: Educational Statesman.* Baltimore: Johns Hopkins University Press, 1983.

Bussing, Charles E., David E. Kromm, and Stephen L. Stover. *Geography at Kansas State University.* Manhattan, KS: Kansas State University, 2007.

Carey, James C. *Kansas State University: The Quest for Identity.* Lawrence, KS: Regents Press of Kansas, 1977.

Chance-Reay, Michaeline. *Land Grant Ladies: Kansas State University Presidential Wives.* Manhattan, KS: Riley County Historical Society, 1999.

Coleman, Richard P., and Virginia Quiring. *A History for Friends of the Kansas State University Libraries…The Association's First Twenty-One Years Beginning 1984.* Manhattan, KS: Friends of K-State Libraries, 2005.

Copeland, Kristin, and Gloria Freeland. *Historical Moments in the Past 100-Plus Years*, JMC Centennial. Manhattan, KS: Kansas State University, 2010.

Cowles, Ina F. *Eighty-four Years of Clothing and Textiles at Kansas State College, 1873-1957.* Manhattan, KS: privately printed, 1957.

Denton, Betty Lou, and Merle L. Eyestone. *Kansas 4-H: The History of Head, Heart, Hands, and Health, 1906-1993.* Manhattan, KS: Kansas 4-H Foundation, 1993.

Donley, Arvin and Meyer Sosland, eds. *The 100th Anniversary of Kansas State University's Department of Grain Science and Industry, 1910-2010.* Kansas City, MO: Sosland Publishing Company, 2010.

Eisenhower, Milton S. *Report to Kansas: An Account of Seven Years of Stewardship.* Manhattan, KS: Kansas State College, 1950.

Elmore, R. G., and Howard H. Erickson. *A Century of Excellence: Kansas State University College of Veterinary Medicine.* Virginia Beach, VA: Donning Company Publishers, 2005.

Farrell, F. D. *Little Essays on Going to College.* N.p., n.d.

_____. *"Prexy Says—": Comments on College Education and Related Topics.* N.p., n.d.

Fischer, Emil C. *Kansas State University: A Walk Through the Campus.* 2nd ed. Manhattan, KS: KSU Foundation, 1992.

Fryer, Holly C. *History of the Development and Activities of the Department of Statistics and Statistical Laboratory at Kansas State College/Kansas State University from 1940-1990.* Manhattan, KS: printed by the author, 1992.

Gibson, Virginia Noah. "The Effect of the Populist Movement on Kansas State Agricultural College." Master's thesis, Kansas State College of Agriculture and Applied Science, 1932. Available online at http://archive.org/details/effectofpopulist00gibs.

Hoeflin, Ruth. *History of a College: From Woman's Course to Home Economics to Human Ecology, 1873-1988, Kansas State University.* Manhattan, KS: College of Human Ecology, Kansas State University, 1988.

Howes, Charles C., ed. *Kansas State University: A Pictorial History, The First Century, 1863-1963.* Manhattan, KS: Kansas State University, 1962.

Janicke, Tim J., Pete Souza, and Jeff A. Taylor, eds. *A Week at K-State: College Life as Seen by 44 Photojournalists from Oct 12–19, 1986.* Manhattan, KS: KSU Student Publications, Inc., 1987.

Jensen, Byron W. "College Music on the Konza Prairie: A History of Kansas State's Department of Music from 1863-1990." PhD dissertation, Kansas State University, 1990. ProQuest (9029272).

Kansas State Agricultural College. *The Inauguration of William Marion Jardine, B. S., LL. D., as President of the Kansas State Agricultural College.* Manhattan, KS: Department of Industrial Journalism and Printing, 1919.

Kansas State College of Agriculture and Applied Science. "Extension Progress," Cooperative Extension Service Bulletin 85 (January 1941).

Kansas State University. *From Concept to Creation: The History and Memories of Your K-State Student Union.* Manhattan, KS: Kansas State University, 2006.

———. *History of the Kansas Extension Service from 1868 to 1964.* Compiled by Earl H. Teagarden. 3 vols. Manhattan, KS: Kansas State University, [1964–1968?].

Kellett, Carol, and Alexandria Teagarden. *Legacy of Leadership: Human Ecology at Kansas State University.* Manhattan, KS: College of Human Ecology, Kansas State University, 2010.

Knutson, Herbert. *A History of the Department of Entomology: Kansas State University, 1879 to 1990.* Manhattan, KS: Department of Entomology, Kansas State University, 1991.

May, Cheryl. *Legacy: Engineering at Kansas State University.* Manhattan, KS: College of Engineering, Kansas State University, 1983.

McCain, James A. *The 1950s at Kansas State University: Report of a Decade of Progress.* Manhattan, KS: Kansas State University, 1960.

McKee, Miles. *Building the Legacy: A History of the Kansas State University Department of Animal Sciences & Industry*. Manhattan, KS: Kansas State University, 2009.

North, Bill, with Brent Jackson and Kate Meyer. *. . . .to build up a rich collection. . . .* Manhattan, KS: The Marianna Kistler Beach Museum of Art, 2003.

Posler, Gerry L., and Gary M. Paulsen, eds. *K-State Agronomy Centennial, 1906-2006: A Century Remembered; A Centennial History of the Department of Agronomy*. Manhattan, KS: Agricultural Experiment Station and Cooperative Extension Service, 2006.

Quiring, Virginia, ed. *The Milton S. Eisenhower Years at Kansas State University*. Manhattan, KS: Friends of the Libraries of Kansas State University, 1986.

Reagan, Charles. *Political Power and Public Influence: The Landon Lectures, 1984-2010*. Manhattan, KS: printed by author, 2011.

Richter, William, and Charles Reagan, eds. *The Landon Lectures: Perspectives from the First Twenty Years*. Manhattan, KS: Friends of the Libraries of Kansas State University, 1987.

Self, Huber. *A History of Geography at Kansas State University*. Manhattan, KS: printed by author, 1983.

Shoop, Robert J. *A University Renaissance: Jon Wefald's Presidency at Kansas State*. Manhattan, KS: Ag Press, 2001.

Stroh, Charles. *Kansas State University, 1980-1990: Department of Art, KSU Friends of Art, and the Marianna Kistler Beach Museum of Art*. Davenport, IA: Fidlar Doubleday, 2012.

Trotter, Don M. *An 80 Year Review, 1905-1985: Kansas State University, College of Veterinary Medicine*. Manhattan, KS: Kansas State University, 1985.

Walters, John Daniel. *History of the Kansas State Agricultural College*. Manhattan, KS: KSAC Printing Department, 1909.

Willard, Julius T. "Bluemont Central College, the Forerunner of Kansas State College." *Kansas Historical Quarterly* 13, no. 4 (May 1945): 323–357.

_____. *History of the Kansas State College of Agriculture and Applied Science*. Manhattan, KS: KSC Press, 1940.

Index

About the Authors

(DM-C&M)

Cliff Hight

Cliff Hight is an assistant professor in the Kansas State University Libraries and has been the university archivist since 2011. His primary stewardship is the preservation and accessibility of university records of enduring value. He has been in the profession since 2005 and holds master's degrees in information science and history from the University at Albany, State University of New York. Cliff and his wife, Lindi, are the parents of four children: Kellen, Leah, Mara, and Brynna. He recognizes their sacrifices while he has been co-authoring his first book and deeply appreciates their patience and support.

(DM-C&M)

Anthony R. Crawford

Anthony R. Crawford was employed as the university archivist of Kansas State University in 1983. After an expansion of the Richard L. D. and Marjorie J. Morse Department of Special Collections in 2011, he assumed the position of curator of manuscripts. He has been a professional archivist since 1973 when he obtained his MLS from the University of Oklahoma. Crawford taught high school history upon earning a BS degree in education from Oklahoma State University in 1967. Among his publications is the *Posters of World War I and World War II in the George C. Marshall Research Foundation* (editor), University Press of Virginia. He holds the academic rank of associate professor and is a charter member of the Academy of Certified Archivists.